I0074596

TALES FROM

THE e–TRENCHES

Why Too Much
Of Our Software
Has Glitches

BY JUDITH C. PAGEL

Copyright © 2016 by Judith C. Pagel

All Rights Reserved

No part of this publication may be reproduced, distributed, or transmitted in any form or by any means, including photocopying, recording, or other electronic or mechanical methods, without the prior written permission of the publisher, except in the case of brief quotations embodied in critical reviews and certain other noncommercial uses permitted by copyright law.

Published by

Cache la Poudre Press, LLC

327 Riva Ridge Dr D105

Fort Collins, CO 80526

ISBN 978–0–9864212–3–5

We have tried to recreate events, locales and conversations from our memories of them. In order to maintain their anonymity in some instances we have changed the names of individuals and places. We may have changed some identifying characteristics and details such as physical properties, occupations and places of residence.

Although the author and publisher have made every effort to ensure that the information in this book was correct at press time, the author and publisher do not assume and hereby disclaim any liability to any party for any loss, damage, or disruption caused by errors or omissions, whether such errors or omissions result from negligence, accident, or any other cause.

Dedication

To Frank, whose thoughts and contributions have enriched this book immeasurably. All my thanks and all my love.

Table of Contents

Chapter 1: Too Many Glitches in our Software

Earlier today, as I sat down at my PC, I was simply going to quick forward an email to my spouse before getting down to book writing. The email was a simple package tracking note for a recent internet purchase. All I needed was to forward this one email to him — he's the family member that follows the adventures of UPS, FEDEX, and USPS so our purchases don't get lost in the cloud.

Now about this email. Hard to do? I would not think so. I have been in high tech since 1966. (For those of you who can remember the first few Super Bowls — I to V — yes, way back then I was using the IBM 1130, the PDP–8, and the IBM 7094 in their days of glory. I started then with computers and have been there through every generation since.) You would think I could forward a simple email.

But before this was over, I was near strangling someone or something. Somebody (those somebodies in the cloud who seem to have complete control over my e–life these days) had changed my email on the last update and I couldn't find "forward" to save my life. So, following the always given advice, I restarted/reloaded the email program — "reload" is IT's equivalent of *"abracadabra"* and is frequently given as the solution to all computer problems —

and what to my wondering eyes should appear but that magic word: "forward".

I don't know how the rest of you feel, but I'm getting more than a little pained by all the software that does not seem to be working these days or at least working the way one expected. Remember having an exciting time trying to sign up for Obamacare? Remember the last time you hit "update" and discovered you would be busy for the next few hours — or did it just seem like days? Remember seeing the words, "Click on button to download" and there was no button?

I'm getting tired of going to the website for a favorite restaurant only to find out that the last time the site was updated was slightly before Paul Revere's famous ride. Or better yet, the page you needed with this week's specials is frozen in space somewhere.

Problems with testing for Common Core are much more frightening. Diane Ravitch reported in the New York Times that computer glitches are common with the testing for Common Core. More than 30 states have reported computer testing problems since 2013.

Finally, these experiences are really bothersome. The future of our world is going to depend more and more each day on our ability to capture all the benefits which computer science offers. We need to do whatever we can to ensure its value.

Why This Book

There is one primary goal for this book. That goal is to examine more carefully why our software keeps

going wrong with alarming frequency or does quirky things. We will use the examination to uncover ways we can improve our software output. What will be covered is real happenings down in the trenches where software applications are born. That was where I worked.

Recently, you have had the opportunity to read about the titans of the tech industry — how they grew up, how they were educated, and how they related to the world.

What you have probably *not* read about or learned about is the inside of the tech industry — down where the software is actually written — down where mistakes are made and before they are corrected.

I would like to take you on a tour of the past half century in high tech from someone actually in the e–trenches. What I saw, I saw from the inside — from those who reported to me and from those to whom I reported. I'm simply one of those guys that prepared the code for much of what we Americans do every day and who later, as a project manager, led coding groups for the types of things we do every day.

If you scratched your head over how the Obamacare software could have taken so long and cost so much, you might have at least some of your questions answered here. You will get a good look inside to see how IT departments work to produce your software. (What may be new to many is taking a good look inside departments where a good program takes a year or more to write and the input of 50–100 coders.)

Is This Book Appropriate for You?

I've written this book to be more directed to those of you who are much less familiar with computer science and programming.

You don't have to know anything about IT/information technology, coding, or programming to have full comprehension of the material.

You will likely be interested in this book if any part of your work success depends on a piece of software. You may be a coder/programmer; you may be a low level or high level manager with little or no coding experience; or you may be a stakeholder in an application written for your department.

As a student or prospective student, you may also be interested in this book in order to learn more about real IT. You may be considering majoring in computer science and you want to learn more about the working world after majoring in computer science.

Finally, and of great importance, you may be a parent interested in your older children's or teens' accomplishments in computing science. My intent is to look at both the good and the bad.

A few closing points: This is not a tell–all book. If it were, I would explicitly identify each corporation talked about. But I'm not writing this book to go after anyone. I am writing this book to help all of us. Moreover, the examples you will see are the kind that could have (and probably already have) happened at many companies.

And one last note. For a person reading this book — regardless of whether you are a student, potential student, or a business manager (think small business, medium business, as well as very large corporation) I will be writing as if you have no background whatsoever in IT. I will really work at this. I Promise.

To repeat: I will write as if you have no background whatsoever in IT. I promise.

In summary, the major reason for this book is to detail (especially for those of you not in e–trenches) my thoughts on how it is and why it is that way too much of our software does not work reliably. In the least, it does not consistently do what we expect it to do. And I'm not even talking here about the numerous hackings of major programs. I'm talking about mistakes — just mistakes — requiring upgrades and more upgrades and more upgrades. (The software vendors do not often tell you what the upgrades are for.) If you have **not** been overwhelmed lately with upgrades, please send your secret along to me and you do not need to read further.

The Layout of the Book

The plans for this book are to give you a tour from the beginning of a very typical major software project through the final publishing and maintenance. As we proceed, at each step we'll cover problem areas where I clearly saw mistakes or their possibility.

Each problem area will be placed in bold font and enclosed within a border. *(You might also want to refer to these enclosed problem statements as "challenges".)* The end of each chapter will include suggestions on how to approach correcting these problems. And finally, when necessary, we will include background information to keep everyone on a level playing field.

Fair warning before we start. Most of the suggestions will *not* be the outcome of revelations of a new and better existence. There will be no leaps to the 22nd century. No, the corrections will simply be common sense and the way you would approach the problem if you were there and thought about it. The reason too many problems do not get fixed in today's world is because no one ever approaches the problem in the first place. And that is truly the case with computing.

My one fear is that you will find me "negative". When that occurs, just remind yourself that the purpose here is to reveal those negatives. So just hang with me, please.

This first section is a little educational catchup. It explains what "coding/programming" is. If you do not need the education, just skip the next chapter. **However, you may be interested before we start that about half of the "bosses" I had during my IT years as a STEM employee were not programmers themselves.**

This section should help parents follow the progress of their kids in becoming computer savvy. This section should also help stakeholders in a software application keep track of what the coders in IT are really doing.

Chapter 2: Intro to Programming

Background: What is Programming

I'm pretty sure that a lot of you have seen announcements lately about getting more of our workers trained in information technology (IT) and/or computer science and/or computer coding. The theory is, of course, that we can replace jobs where workers have been laid off with jobs in the "technologies of tomorrow" and everyone will be happy. (Don't tell me you missed this note from the politicians.)

But, **if** IT is so wonderful, it sure is hard to understand why these days our computers seem to us to spend more time getting "updated" then they spend actually "running", why it now seems to take an eternity for "ads" to load onto an internet page, why too much of the time the internet page we really want to see does not exist or we cannot find it, and finally, why our kids do *not* seem to be enthusiastically mentioning possible careers in computer science. Things just seem to be a little "off" in too many places.

I decided to write this book so I could address at least some of the problems I witnessed in my time as an IT worker. My hopes were to clean things up just a bit to get the younger workers more interested in computer science and make life a bit easier for all of us. At the very least, I thought maybe I could suppress the all too frequent screams from my spouse's end of the apartment as he measures his beard growth while waiting for the latest update to finish.

I will be honest, though. My concerns are larger than the ones above. My fear is that if we do not do some clean up, we are soon going to join the countries we used to refer to as "non–industrialized". We are currently being left behind too many countries in terms of the technological expertise of both our students and our workers.

However, at this point in designing the book, I did run into a little bit of a show stopper. One of the reasons we do not get things cleaned up faster is that computer coding/programming is one of those esoteric topics understood only by those who are computer savvy. We all need to understand at least the problem areas even if we do not become the world's most accomplished programmers. We can do that if we level the field and give all of us a relatively simple understanding of computer programming. The next section is going to present a brief tutorial on "what programming is."

Not to worry. The section is short and written for those with no background in IT. One of the most interesting parts about the origin and history of computers and programming is how it got started.

How Computers Changed our World

In the olden days before computers, our math labs were filled with Friden calculators (read very big adding machines — that's *desktop size* big) — or for those really

8

advanced — electronic calculators. If you wanted the sum of three numbers, you entered those three numbers and then hit "sum" to get the sum. If the numbers changed, you would enter all three numbers all over again.

Then came what is a simple, simple idea but one which has virtually changed our world forever. With a personal computer (pc), we can provide the pc with "machine instructions" to tell the computer what to do next (such as add 2 + 4). But — and this is the idea: **Give the machine instructions but use variable names instead of numbers in those instructions** (i.e., Add num1 + num2). Then when you want to run the program, you can have the computer replace the variable names with the actual numbers you want to use in their place *for that run* — num1 = 2 and num2 = 4, now add num1 + num2.) (Note: You are the one who makes up the variable names. The machine makes the substitutions for you.)

Note that you can change the values for each of the variables for the next run, and the next run, etc. In other words, write the program once, and use that program many, many times with many, many sets of numbers.

What I'd like to do is begin by showing you one of the earlier computer languages — Fortran, which was introduced in 1954. Compared to today's languages, Fortran is simple and straightforward.

Important: I have referred so far to "programming". It is also called "coding", and I will use that term too. I also will include in our discussions additional software (like databases, for storing data, for example) and hardware (like

9

server networks) which together make the whole "programming" idea work.

An Example of Fortran Programming

Below is a simple program written in Fortran. Fortran was used heavily in the 1950's and 1960's and is still frequently used for main frame (the largest computers) programming and for super computers with parallel processing.

The program below figures the final grade for students in such and such a math class. Assume there are three mid–term exams (Midtrm1, Midtrm2, etc.). The first step in getting the final grade is to average the three mid–terms — call it mid–term average (MidAver). Then the final grade is itself the average of the final exam and the mid–term average (Final). The program calculates the final grade and then prints it for every student in the class. When all the student averages have been calculated, the program calculates and prints a class average (ClasAver).

PROGRAM Grades

IMPLICIT NONE

INTEGER NumStud, StudNum, NumClas

REAL MidTrm1, MidTrm2, MidTrm3, Final

REAL MidAver, FnlAver, ClasAver

REAL PassMrk

PassMrk = 65.0

ClasAver = 0.0

READ (*,*) NumStud

DO NUMCLAS = 1, NumStud

  READ (*,*) StudNum, Midtrm1, Midtrm2, Midtrm3, Final

  MidAver = (Midtrm1 + Midtrm2 + Midtrm3)/3.0

  FnlAver = (MidAver + Final)/2.0

  WRITE (*,*) 'Student # = ', StudNum

  IF (FnlAver >= PassMrk) THEN

    WRITE (*,*) 'Student passes. Score = ', FnlAver

  ELSE

    WRITE (*,*) 'Student fails. Score = ', FnlAver

  END IF

  ClasAver = ClasAver + FnlAver

END DO

  ClasAver = ClasAver /NumStud

  Write (*,*) "Class average is ", ClasAver

END PROGRAM Grades

Step by Step Through the Fortran Program

For this program, we start by coming up with a variable name for all the figures we need to produce the averages (Midtrm1/Midtrm2/etc.) and for the averages themselves (MidAver/FnlAver/etc.).

11

1. **Fortran is very picky. It needs to know for each of these variable names, before you start, whether the variable will be an integer — INTEGER — or a floating point number (has a decimal point) — REAL.** *The statement "IMPLICIT NONE" is used to inhibit a very old feature of Fortran that by default treats all variables that start with the letters i, j, k, l, m and n as integers.*

2. **The READ and WRITE statements tell the computer what variables to read in or write out,** *and — in place of the two *'s in one version — where to find them (an input/output file or tape number) and what format the numbers are in (number of decimal points).*

3. **To actually run the program, an input file or tape or (in the past) a deck of cards will be included with the program.** *It will have the number of students on the first line or card — READ (*,*) NumStud. Then subsequent cards/lines in the file will each have a student number (StudNum) followed by his or her four grades. Let us say that the first line in the input file has "2" = two students. The second line has 1, 67, 75, 88, and 89. The first time through the DO loop, the program puts 67 into Midtrm1 for Student #1, 75 into Midterm2, 88 into Midtrm3, and 89 into Final.*

4. **Fortran has instructions that allow you to Jump to a certain line (for example, GO TO), to repeat a set of lines over and over until some criteria has been met (DO to END DO), or to take some action IF or WHEN a specific criterion has been met.**

WITH THE EXCEPTION OF THESE JUMP OR REPEAT TYPE OF STATEMENTS, ALL OF THE INSTRUCTIONS ARE CARRIED OUT LINEARLY — FROM THE FIRST LINE OF THE PROGRAM UNTIL THE LAST.

5. **The way that statements in Fortran work is that they are telling you to "replace what is on the left side of the equal sign with what is on the right side of the equal sign."** *That equal sign up there does not mean that what is item on the left is "equal to" what is on the right. Otherwise we would have a really strange statement that "ClasAver = ClasAver + FnlAver", especially when FnlAver is greater than zero.*

6. A very frequent item in Fortran is "i = i + 1" or a similar one that is used in those repeating statements to give you a count of how many times you have repeated the statement so far. Before starting a segment of code that needs repeating for each student in the class, for example, one would set i = 0. Then, each time through this code segment, the value of "i"

13

would be increased by "1" until one would reach the number of students, n. Then you quit going through that segment of code. Again, the way that statements in Fortran work is that they are telling you to "replace what is on the left side of the equal sign with what is on the right side of the equal sign."

7. **Note: Points 5 and 6 may be the single hardest part of programming to understand and work with.** *And it is hard to teach. What I used to do when teaching (even to graduate students) would be to have the class start by marking a set of boxes, each with the name of one of the variables. Then we would go through the program line by line and actually move numbers from one box to another to see how the Fortran statements and, particularly, "i = i + 1" really work.*

8. **Second, of great importance, punctuation is really important in these languages**. *Leave out the comma and the program won't work. Put in an "i" instead of a "1" and the program won't work. As I told you, I have spent days upon occasion trying to find that "mistake". When I was learning Fortran, our machine was kind enough to print out a picture of Alfred E. Neuman from Mad Magazine when we made too many mistakes.*

9. **Finally, the program presented above is simple. In the real world however, things will usually not be that simple.** *The program to calculate final grades will probably not stand alone but be a part of a total educational system to keep track of students, their grades, and the faculty, all in a couple of databases and all part of a network system to help distribute the results. Our example, however, should give you a start.*

Fair Warning: What Programming Is Not

I know there are many of you who just never became proficient in computer programming yourselves, but who nevertheless are proud of their kids who use computers regularly and have become quite proficient in producing presentations and major written pieces. I am sure you have seen their Power Point presentations and/or their Microsoft Word documents.

Some of what you may have seen may not always have been "programming" per se. What you may have seen is the equivalent of an "app" the kids have on their phone or of something like a media remote control. (Microsoft's Power Point, Word, Excel, and Access are "applications".)

Applications can be very sophisticated and can require much experience to learn, but they are not programming languages. The reason is that for applications, **someone else has** *already programmed* **the remote or the app to take specific actions when specific buttons are pushed.**

15

To give you an example of an app, let us say you have opened Microsoft WORD. You will see a blank page. You can start typing. At some point, highlight one word — say "computer". You highlight by positioning the mouse on the "c" and then, holding down the left side, dragging the mouse through the word "computer". If you then move the mouse to the HOUSE menu item "**B**" and click on the "**B**", the word "computer" will go into bold type. **Using similar point and click routines**, you can italicize sections, set margins, insert page numbers, etc., etc., etc.

If your kids are younger (below 11 or 12) they may have been exposed mainly to applications. When it comes to "programming", there are a fair number of computer professionals who feel that kids should not be taught computer languages until they are at least in middle school. Real analytical skills often don't start appearing in kids until the early teens. So don't be upset if you see "applications" instead of "programming".

I did feel it necessary, however, to make the distinction. While *some* jobs are available for those with solid experience in applications (such as Access in Microsoft Office or in web design, such as Dreamweaver or for computer–aided design such as AutoCAD), most job openings are for those with specific programming languages under their belt.

If your kids are in middle school, it may be time to introduce them to programming. Just remember one thing. Computers should always be fun. Your kids will be living with them for the rest of their lives. It should be a happy arrangement.

Later you will find that there will be days on the less happy side. The programming for my thesis put me on one occasion ready to quit everything and just eat chocolate for the next decade. Would you believe that I had typed a "1" instead of an "I" in one instruction? (If you are having trouble deciphering what I just wrote, I had actually typed a number when I should have typed a capital letter.)

It took a mere four days to find that error in 300 pages of code – and 300 pages tends to be a small program.

Chapter 3: Too Many Languages

Background.

This chapter, for the first time, is going to look at problem areas/challenges. They will be in bold type and boxed. The first area to look at will be to examine the languages themselves.

In Chapter 1, we looked at one of the early programming languages, Fortran. Over the years, many different programming languages were developed for specific uses:

> • The most popular now for basic programming are C and variants thereof (C++, C#), Java (J2EE and Java SE 6), and Visual Basic (VB 6 and VB.NET).

> • The other "basic" program is HTML (now up to HTML5) which presents information on a web page along with its helper CSS.

> • JavaScript allows a programming language to be integrated into HTML.

Then there are program languages and application frameworks which meet a specific need. Several have to do with databases:

> • SQL is the language used to access data from most large system databases.

• Access is a Microsoft application which is basically a database management system. It uses a Data Window which makes it really easy to read data from a database. It actually writes the SQL statement for you.

• PowerBuilder (a language, not used as much today as before) has a Data Window which (similar to the one in Access) makes it really easy to read data from a database.

• Apache Struts 2 is an open–source (free to everyone) web application framework for developing Java EE applications for the web. The framework offers ways to make the programming easier. For example, it will retrieve data from a database table, and insert it into to a web page.

There are other languages for other needs:

• PHP is open source and is used to develop web applications which have an interaction between the Web Application and the Users (i.e., it can access information typed into a web form and do something with it).

• And then there are the 30 or so languages specifically for mobile devices/smartphones, such as Ruby, with its Framework Ruby on Rails, and Objective–C.

Most really good programmers can program in a number of these languages. Or they can learn a new one in a couple of weeks. (On my last resume, I listed 11 languages).

The reason that programmers can use so many languages is that underneath it all, the base instructions (arithmetic statements, DO, WHEN, IF, etc.) are in every one of the languages. They also tend to look very much alike. In fact, often the primary difference among them is the punctuation. And this punctuation is the bugaboo of all programmers. We have all wasted hours and days looking for the code error when it actually is a missing semi–colon which is the cause of many depressive episodes.

I explained before that underneath it all, the base instructions in almost all languages are the same. Caution: They do punctuate differently. Below are the same statements in Visual Basic, Java, and C#, using the WHILE instruction.

vb.NET

```
While interest_year < interest_period
    base = base + (rate * base)
    interest_year +=1
    End While
```

Java

```
While (interest_year < interest_period)
    {
    base = base + (rate * base);
    interest_year ++;
    }
```

C#

While (interest_year < interest_period)

```
    {
    base = base + (rate*base);

    interest_year += 1;

    }
```

All three languages have shortcuts for line 3 that mean the same thing as interest_year = interest_year + 1. We used the shortcuts in the examples above:

VB.NET interest_year += 1

Java interest_year ++;

C# interest_year += 1; OR interest_year ++;

And do remember — in the real world, forget that semi–colon in Java or C# and the program simply won't run.

Problem Areas: Too Many Complicated Languages/Too Much Punctuation

And now we are down to the first reason so much of our software doesn't work, at least from my point of view. Basically we have too many complicated languages. First of all, we waste too much time correcting punctuation.

It is only fair to tell you that some IDE's will produce an outline/a layout of the code required, which does help with the punctuation problem. (An IDE — Integrated Development Environment — is a software application that provides facilities to

22

computer programmers for software development such as a code editor, help in debugging/finding errors, and ways to automate the programming.)

> **Problem: Basically we have too many complicated languages. We waste too much time correcting punctuation, which in many cases is the only difference between some statements in different languages. We end up focusing on the grammar rather than the function of the code.**

Okay, we now see that getting training in one of the three leading basic languages is really, really hard. But that gets compounded by the 15 or so other "new" languages. Oh yes, I have barely mentioned the 30 or so new languages for mobile.

Insert Another Language

Below is a second example of yet another situation that can happen when there are too many languages. One scene occurred right before the dot com bubble burst. While I started with highly skilled bosses in this department, later on, a project manager was moved in between us and the bosses. This manager did not have high level programming skills.

At the same time, several PowerBuilder programmers were brought in for a special project. Word through the department had it that PowerBuilder programmers at that time were going for something around $150 per hour, which means that the company was spending around $300 per hour with a contracting firm to hire each programmer.

There was one small problem here. In talking to the guys and seeing their work, I found out that they had used PowerBuilder *only* at the very beginning to access data from the database. *PowerBuilder made the data pulls easy.*

The rest of the time they were programming in Java, for which one would *not* tend to pay anywhere near $150 per hour. Because the Project Manager did not have programming skills in either of the two languages, the overpayment was not noticed. I did tell her.

Lack of documentation really causes problems around later updates because coders miss the code section that was done in other languages and they don't make the needed changes or they don't even understand what the added programming does.

> **Problem, Extended: To repeat, we have too many languages. The vast number alone makes it difficult for computer science departments to control what languages are actually being used.**

> The too many languages problem gets even worse when programs need to be updated and no one still working in the department knows that an additional language is hiding in the code.

Alternative Solutions

Solid documentation of how the program is being written and what is included will help solve the "too many languages" problem. There will be times when a particular language is set up in such a way that it is ideal for certain tasks (say, for example, something like character manipulation.) In this case, it is actually more efficient to use the new language — **so long as it is documented.**

An additional solution arises out of my realization while working on this project that the *only* persons who ever examined the code as it was being written were the coders – those doing the programming.

We never had anyone examining the code from an "uninterested" point of view. Of importance, what we did have was a big enough department that it could support an independent "code reviewer" whose job it would be to look at everyone's code.

What the reviewer would look for is good code organization and proper use of the selected language and examples of hidden code in another language.

One other possible solution comes out of programming for the internet. Whereas there are many languages for programming personal computers, the internet is different. The main language here is HTML5. There is really only one language for writing directly to the web. The language is kept up by an independent group, the *W3Schools* group. The language is kept very simple.

(Adding the JavaScript language will allow one to add some programming to the HTML.) Again, things are kept simple. Nothing needs to be done to take advantage of this HTML/JavaScript solution. Just learn and enjoy!

Summary of Problem Areas

Basically we have too many languages. We waste too much time correcting punctuation, which in many cases is the only difference between some statements in different languages.

To repeat, we have too many languages. The vast number alone makes it difficult for computer science departments to control what languages are actually being used by its coders. This difficulty grows when programs need to be updated, e.g., a change in tax laws, personnel systems, additional reports, etc.

Chapter 4: Learning a Language

Our Kids Deserve a Solid Programming Background

Think for a moment about where we come across "programming" in our daily lives. To start, when we go to the automatic teller for our money, programming is behind what the automatic teller is doing. When we pick up those tickets for the ball game, programming is behind Ticketmaster and StubHub. When we go to Zillow to look at a possible new house, programming is behind "the street view." Even when we go to the grocery store to get veggies, programming is behind the veggie order. When we — oh heck, try to find someplace these days where programming is *not* behind it. And don't even think about the space in databases needed for all those items being sold by Amazon and others on the "Internet of Things." And we haven't even mentioned Artificial Intelligence (Hi, Cortana? Have you met Siri yet?).

What is more, each day we find more and more ways to bring that programming in. The advertising business is now fully developing advertising for the internet — all kinds and in all ways. You see, Facebook, as I write this, just turned in fabulous quarterly results. What you need to know is that basically, essentially all of Facebook's income comes from guess what — advertising. (And you thought — okay, hoped — that advertising would die out as we moved from static TV to the mobile life.) As I write this, the advertising heads are looking frantically to find big data analysts and programmers so they can further improve mobile advertising's results. (Note: That reminds me of how I got into advertising a few thousand years ago, but it was for tv advertising.)

So, even if your child is going into art history or sports management or something else non–scientific, there is still a strong case that their performance, regardless of the field, could improve if they were given a good feel for what programming is. What may not be widely "programmed" today may lead to a lot of work for programmers in the near future. And programming is even more important if your child is going into a field like science or engineering where programming is used every day.

The only hard part now will be to find a way to get your kids exposed to a good programming course. That may be a little harder. You may want to try something easy instead, like playing a game of GO with IBM's Watson computer.

Problem Area: A Good Course is Hard to Find

As I noted before, the best estimate is that 90% of our high schools do not teach computer programming.

There is a big problem here.

http://www.huffingtonpost.com/hadi-and-ali-partovi/teach-coding-schools_b_2759066.html

The problem is for high schools to be able to find someone — anyone — *capable* of teaching a major programming course. A friend of mine announced the other day that she was getting a "Masters" in computer science. Later I found out that she was learning Microsoft Office (Word, PowerPoint, Access, Excel) in order to teach these at the local high school. The most pitiful case was the group of students at the *same* local high school who had formed an after school group to teach themselves Java — if you can't find any other way.

> **Problem: The hard part these days is to find a way to get our kids exposed to good programming courses. The best estimate is that 90% of our high schools don't teach computer programming.**

One of the best school districts in the country with which I'm familiar provides a 9–week course teaching every conceivable aspect of computing, from Google Search to Internet Safety to Google Docs to Data Analysis to Web Page Design to Intro to Programming. You might guess, however, that in that nine weeks, students are truly getting a "once over lightly" introduction to each of these subjects.

Just to make us truly feel good, a study conducted in October 2014 among 20 European Ministries of Education, found that computer programming and coding is already part of the curriculum in 12 countries: Bulgaria, Cyprus, Czech

Republic, Denmark, Estonia, Greece, Ireland, Italy, Lithuania, Poland, Portugal and the UK (England). Seven more countries also plan to integrate the topic into their curricula in the future.

http://www.eun.org/publications/detail?publicationID=481

Back to the real world — try going into any small to medium size U.S. community these days. Try to find a good set of courses in any of several programming languages. You may get one course or two at a local community college — it is hard to find one or two *individual* courses anywhere else.

There will also be one or two courses at major universities but most universities will require you to *register as a full–time student.* Just by looking around, I came to the conclusion that most of the universities will either teach C or Java or one of the two open source (that means free to everyone) languages: PHP or Python. (Open source denotes free software for which the original source code is made freely available and may be redistributed and modified.) Most universities will teach one, at most two, languages.

Now that we've been through the community, let us look at the wider U.S. First and very important, what we *do not* see in this world is the companies who devised these programs (Oracle Sun for Java, Microsoft for Visual Basic.Net, and C at Bell Labs/now Alcatel Lucent) also providing massive courses for students to learn them. We do not see many of these courses now. *We did not see many of these courses years ago.* This situation is in stark contrast to India, where three major companies have trained many,

many coders. The main companies there are Tata, Infosys, and Wipro. These three companies were among the top companies receiving H–1B visas in recent years.

> **Problem: The major language developers — Microsoft and Sun Java —— have not in general been at the forefront in providing courses for students to learn these languages. It is very difficult in the U.S. to find individual courses in the major computer languages.**

Possible Solutions

Below are a couple of learning sources for those lucky enough to live in the right cities. If you are one of the lucky ones, a complete set of courses in Java tends to be available at a series of firms used by large companies to train their personnel. These courses will not be for everyone. These courses are expensive — starting at well over $2000 per course. (I'm not talking Phoenix or the like. I'm talking about private companies like Quilogy Services from Aspect, an Oracle Training University in St. Charles, MO, whose sole business is teaching the higher level computer classes for business.) Some of these types of businesses do offer courses to the general public. Others will only offer programs to businesses.

Finally, in some cities you may really luck out and find a source like the University of Missouri at St. Louis.

Shortly before the turn of the century, my husband and I knew we were going to have to make a career change. Computing was very hot because Y2K changes were needed for many computer programs (i.e., changing 1999 something to 2000 something). We did need to get our own computer skills state of the art. Over the next few years we each spent about $10,000 each taking a variety of computer courses at the computer center at the University of Missouri at St. Louis. The program was (and still is) more than excellent.

The program name is the Computer Education & Training Center at the University of Missouri at St. Louis. For between $300 and $500 per course, one can take courses in basic office skills (Word, Excel, Access, Power Point) as well as in quite a few languages (from JavaScript to Java to VB.NET to PHP to SQL) plus courses in digital publishing. Do check all the colleges and junior colleges around you to see if any are offering a program like the one at UMSL.

We came out with Chancellor's Certificates: On the Computer (2003); In Web Programming/Databases (2003); and In Web Page Design (2006). As I said, the program is still running. It may be important to note that most of the students in these classes were male. And at least a third and usually more than that were men 40+ years of age. Today's costs would be about $18,000 for each of us.

If luck is with you, you may live in one of those communities that provides teaching like the Quilogy and UMSL courses above. However, if your town is like too much of the U.S., those programs are just not easy to find.

Finally, you can learn online — even from Harvard. You may also want to look at Lynda.com or Kahnacademy.com, although I tend to recommend a couple of instructor–led courses before moving online.

Alternative Solutions

One solution that we need more of is for those of us in the community to begin to put pressure on our school districts and community colleges to invest in these courses. Here's hoping that this book may make more persons aware of how difficult it is to get the courses and how valuable they are.

Of course, in order for the pressure to work, we also need to use our tax dollars to get more possible teachers into the systems. That will most likely involve federal programs, as opposed to local school districts. (Think of the NDEA Title IV act that was used in the 1960's to produce more college teachers.)

Summary of Problem Areas

The only hard part will be to find a way to get your kids exposed to a good programming course. The best estimate is that 90% of our high schools don't teach computer programming.

The major language developers – Microsoft and Sun Java — have not in general been at the forefront in providing courses for students to learn these languages. It is very difficult in the U.S. to find individual courses in the major computer languages.

Chapter 5: Getting That IT Job

In this chapter I am going to examine just how difficult or easy it is to acquire a programmer's job, from an entry level position to quite high up. You may be tempted to start by asking just how is it that hiring policies can possibly affect the overall excellence of the software produced, but I think what impressed me most was how difficult it was to get my skills in the front door. Too much of my probability of success vs. failure was due to the skills (or lack thereof) of the recruiters looking for someone to hire. Too often they would not recognize high skill levels when presented with such a resume.

So, perhaps the most straightforward way in which hiring can affect the quality of the software produced is by affecting the quality of the personnel who eventually get hired. When the best are not hired, the quality of the software is affected.

Once getting that computer science job is covered, I will move — in Chapters 5–8 to looking at the actual development of a software program — from the beginning planning stages out to the final testing. But first, let's get that job.

Background

It was in the late 1990's that IT and computer science really started to blossom. (They hit their height just in time to produce the bursting of the dot–com bubble at the turn of the century where we needed to get dates from 1999 to 2000.) It was during this broader period that my husband and I were facing how we could get one of the IT jobs for which we had just taken advanced training to update our skills. Timing is everything you know.

In those days, we had not yet heard of LinkedIn or Zip–Recruiter. Before the turn of the century, most companies used to hire their own IT personnel. However, this quickly became very inefficient. One day you needed Java programmers. The next day you needed programmers in another language, like COBOL. The day after that you needed a system architect or a network security specialist.

Small IT firms came to the rescue. These small firms would hire the programmers. Then when a company needed a particular type of programmer, the small IT firm would contract the programmer out to the company who needed that type of programmer.

When a particular type of coder was not needed, the small IT firm would put the coder to work on a major application which the firm was writing for its own benefit, like one for health care or vision care. In case you are interested, when you go to the doctor or eye doctor or dentist, even today, the doctors are probably using one of the business software packages for specific parts of the medical profession that were originally written by one of these small contracting firms.

Unfortunately, over the long haul, this organization was not a profitable one. Coders were not being contracted out enough of the time. Soon, most of these contracting firms existed only to find personnel that companies needed — for time periods as short as 3 months to full time employees. Contract workers were only taken on when they had a placement. Contract workers also tended to be laid off the minute the placement project was completed.

Problem Areas: Getting Hired

Unless things dramatically change in the future, there will be a few 6–foot concrete walls in your way — much like a lot of career paths these days:

At first the recruiters at the contracting firms were skilled in IT and in many languages, systems, and applications. They were like something we called Executive Recruiters of the 1980's, who only exist now for very highly paid positions. These Executive Recruiters were able to recognize a person with higher level skills. Later on — by approximately 2006 — and from my point of view — too many contract recruiters were less skilled in IT and more skilled in personnel issues.

> **Problem: When more than a few contract company recruiters lack skills in computer science and programming and they are the ones selecting prospects for open positions, it becomes just that much more difficult for a prospect trained in an American college or vocational institution to get an IT job and that much more difficult for the employer to hire the best prospect.**

One last point and that is how the contracting firms worked with us. When a large firm in town had a need for a programmer of a certain type, the firm would contact one of the small contracting firms and that contracting firm would list the job description on a job hunting site on the internet. We would spend considerable time browsing all the job hunting sites. *(Monster.com* and *careerbuilder.com* were two we used a lot).

If I understand the contract situation today, in addition to internet sites, these firms now get help from Zip–Recruiter, who posts their opening to a hundred sites and then presents a list of personnel culled from the sites to the firm that needs to hire. The job hunter today also gets help from LinkedIn, by being able to openly present their resume to any and all interested parties.

Before going further describing contract recruiting, there is one other major way to get a computer science job in business. Each spring many larger companies hire a group of students with recent undergrad and graduate degrees from research universities. These students are highly skilled and will hopefully rise quickly within their organizations.

> **Problem: Because many companies tend to resist hiring *directly* unless the prospect has just completed a bachelor's degree or above from a research university, a prospect without that degree will likely have a very small chance of being hired directly by that company.**

Back then, for the rest of us and for many computer scientists, looking for a local IT job was somewhat like trying to get a job at Microsoft or Google. The press used to report that these tech companies were receiving thousands of resumes a day. Computer programs were used to skim the words in a resume to see if they matched any of the words in the job descriptions. We could have sent Microsoft a thousand resumes and we never would have heard from them. (Actually we did send a few resumes to Microsoft, but it wasn't a thousand. And of course we never ever got an acknowledgement for any of our applications.)

Later in our careers, the local recruiters from the contracting firms were carefully checking our resumes for the right words. In two instances where a recruiter got me an interview, I had to go in and explain to the employer that I did not have the proper background for their job description. The recruiter just did not know enough to make the distinction. And word matching had not helped. Because of the problem above, many recruiters seemed hesitant to place us in any position that we had not previously held, which made it even more difficult to get a job.

> **Problem: All along, one of the biggest problems in getting hired for an IT job has been a hesitance on the part of contract company recruiters to recommend anyone for a position the prospect has not previously held. This can be a particularly serious problem for those going after their first job.**

Two other problems. Note that the middle of this IT period of ours was also known as the Great Recession.

Frequently we would get all excited because it would appear that more jobs were opening up. What we quickly learned was that one of the very large corporations had *one* new IT position — one position that they had given to 8 to 10 (or even more) different contracting firms. Talk about misguided exuberance.

> **Problem: Often one corporation may give one job contract to as many as ten or more contracting firms. If too many recruiting firms/ contracting firms are carrying the same job, it is easy to get misled into thinking the market is hotter than it is. This practice in recruiting may also have caused and may still be causing overestimates in the number of IT positions listed by groups like the Labor Department.**

The other problem had to do with "the interview". Remember that I was in my late 50's at that time. Also at that time one of the leading management "theories" focused on the idea that "the team" was all important to the productivity of the group. Interviews were set up with the programming teams, to make sure the prospective employee would fit in well. Unfortunately, the "team" was too often a group of 20–29 year–old males. A friend of mine noted that, unlike his interviews outside IT, these at times felt like and operated like a fraternity or sorority blackball session. I knew the minute I walked into one of these interviews with six 20–year–old's that my chances of getting hired could be as much as one in a thousand.

> **Problem: If you are asked to interview with the "programming team", be aware that your chances of being hired might be very, very small unless you are demographically similar to "the team". In my experience, that most frequently translates to a 20–29 year–old male.**

The situation above is one I got altogether too used to. A colleague of mine came away boiling after being asked in an interview how skilled he was in bowling. The coding team was short someone for their bowling team.

Even in the midst of our IT careers, it took us on average six months to find the next placement. (After finding that many big IT firms were turning over too many full–time employees and replacing them with contract players, several recommendations came about from lawsuit outcomes and Labor Department directives. What this led to was the situation that many of our local companies would not hire a contract player for more than two years without them being made a full time employee.)

(https://www.littler.com/term-limits-contingent-workers-urban-legend-or-necessary-fix)

> **Problem: In my experience, due to Department of Labor recommendations and lawsuit outcomes, most companies would allow contract workers to only work for a firm for two years.**

I cannot be sure how frequently these directives are being followed today or by how many companies, but there are indications they are still in use, although there may be broad differences in how the directives are applied. And while time limits on contract workers and H–1B's may shift from time to time, some sort of time limits are likely to exist for many more years.

I'm going to break in here with a comment. When we became unemployed, there was always the question of whether we should go after another IT job which might take 6 months or more but would pay $25 an hour (i.e., $50,000 a year). Alternatively, we could go to a big box and get a job right away but it would pay half that. So you made the same regardless of whether you were unemployed for six months and had a job for six months or whether you had a job paying half that for 12 months. The trouble with the 12–month job was that once you had that job it would be almost impossible to get back to a job in IT. Can you imagine an IT department enthusiastically hiring someone who had been stocking shelves at Walmart? (By the way, try comparing all of this to the 60% greater salary I made in advertising 20 years earlier, in the 1980's.) Does this help in justifying why we "chose" to remain unemployed?

> **Problem: Almost by definition, and due in part to lawsuit outcomes and federal directives on contract workers, contract workers in the past tended to be employed for two years and then were unemployed for the next six months while they looked for the next contract position.**

When Frank and I started our working days, we thought we had achieved the "American Dream" due to our two full–time salaries. We did not know then, nor did most people, that salaries were dropping enough that soon it would take two working full time to make a decent living. We are still there today.

> **Problem: There's one other exasperating problem for the person trying to get an IT job. That problem is the large number of H–1B's standing in**

> **line in front of them (i.e., foreign workers hired when US. workers are supposedly not available).**
>
> ---
>
> **U.S. companies who work with H–1B's frequently have contracts with programming and recruiting firms that specialize in providing H–1B labor. These programming/ recruiting firms push for additional slots for their foreign personnel.**

The H–1B VISA program was set up to allow the U.S. to bring into the country a certain number of highly skilled workers each year so long as the pay was equal to the current pay for the position and so long as a U.S. citizen could *not* be found to fill the job. (The program, however, does allow our firms to take advantage of foreign worker availability.)

These H–1B workers have a distinct advantage over us. Large firms (three of the four largest are in India) have trained thousands of bright young men and women in computer science, especially coding and programming. At first these men and women work in closely supervised groups in their home city. These groups are doing projects for various firms, many outside the home city. Then, the programmers at the top of the heap are allowed to take on contract positions in the U.S. and other countries. However, unlike most of us in the U.S., they can say that they have *previously worked in that position for an outside client.* (See the closely supervised groups in the home city above.) We in the U.S. normally can't refer to "our previous experience in this type of position" at the beginning of our careers.

It is also helpful to know that the H–1B's tend to come in at the "bottom" of the salary scale for that position and that they will likely not get raises nor expect to be offered a position as an employee. They do have the advantage in many cases of being able to reduce costs for the U.S. firm hiring computer personnel.

Alternative Solutions

While we hear a lot about H–1B visas, it is important to recognize that the best estimate I could come up with is that only 20% of our domestic IT workers are imported on H–1B visas. There should still be openings available for those with programmer and software developer skills. It is important to remember that higher level software developers are currently very much in demand and are expected to remain that way for the near future.

http://www.cringely.com/2012/10/23/what-americans-dont-know-about-h-1b-visas-could-hurt-us-all/

As for providing solutions to the other problems listed above, (such as "team" interviewing or a prospect not having worked in a specific position) sometimes **simply having knowledge of where the pitfalls are** will be as much help as anything else. What a prospect needs to do is make sure his or her expectations match what is happening in the real world. If you know that several firms will have the same contract job, you will not be so upset when too many jobs go away in one day.

I do not expect the H–1B problem to change much in the near future, so long as their biggest cheerleaders are some of the leading technology companies in Silicon Valley. Actually, however, if we Americans can solve the problem of getting more of our youth well educated in computer science and programming, we will in part alleviate the "need" for bringing in more from out of the country. And we will help retain the U.S. technology and scientific lead.

Additional Note:

There exists one final problem in getting hired. The management team responsible for hiring you may not be completely put together. My all–time memorable interview took quite a while to start. (Actually, it never did start.) It seems all those whispered conversations going on in the hallway were the managers deciding what to do with me since the company had laid off my prospective boss 20 minutes before I arrived. Inexplicably, I did not get the job.

Chapter 6: Initial Design: The Waterfall Method

Chapters Two and Three began by showing a simple example of a programming language. Chapter Four covered how one would go about getting into a program to learn one of the programming languages. Chapter Five provided some of some of the best places for getting hired as a coder and some of the places where our IT hiring may not be designed to attract and hold the best personnel.

At this point, however, let us turn to actually getting the program underway and the coding designed. Amazingly, there is an incredible amount of work done for a program long before any coder puts pen to paper. **Even more amazing, one of the biggest contributors to "glitches" occurs as part of the pre–work, i.e., we're piling up the updates before we ever put that pen to paper.**

I am going to use as an example a project in which I was involved as Project Manager. It is a pretty standard example of projects in many corporations. The program was meant to be Enterprise–wide/Corporation–wide and was programmed in J2EE (Java for Enterprise projects).

Chapters Six and Seven will examine the pre–work from a very general point of view, applicable to most departments. Chapters Eight and Nine will describe happenings on a more personal level.

These four chapters will provide many examples of places where the software itself and our procedures produced even more of our all–famous glitches. But do be aware we did complete the project and left it in working order, so be aware that most of our glitches can be handled.

Background: Initial Planning

The best way to begin talking about the actual design and coding of our project (and many others) is to describe the Full Life Cycle Program for designing software. This is the program we used. It is also the program used in some form by most computer science departments for projects, once they get to around medium size.

The actual method used for this project was called "Waterfall". The Waterfall method originated in the manufacturing and construction industries and is one variant of the Full Life Cycle Program.

With the Waterfall method, one designs the entire program before any coding is done. One moves from step to step without ever going backward — much like the water in a waterfall. Should an error be discovered late in the program, Waterfall requires that one go back to the beginning to re–design everything. The following steps are frequently included in descriptions of Waterfall: requirements analysis, design, implementation, testing, installation, and maintenance.

Requirements analysis. Requirements analysis is the first step in a project. This step is quite important because it involves gathering information about the customer needs and defining, in the clearest possible terms, the problem that the product is expected to solve.

As a part of Requirements Analysis, The *Business Analyst* meets with Stakeholders to the program (those who will use and/or depend on the program) in order to determine what characteristics are desired in the new program — what do they need the program to do? The *Requirements Lead* meets with some portion of all those involved to determine particular options and characteristics that would be required, such as the number of expected users and how that number might grow or the necessity of using a specific database, etc. These two issues become a part of defining the goals and objectives of the project.

Often it also involves writing a "vision" statement. The "vision" statement is a concise statement in everyday English that lays out exactly what the program should accomplish. In some departments, the vision statement is written by the stakeholders. In others it is written as a first step by the IT group.

Design. At this point the project moves to the design phase of development. The *Technical Architect* is involved in looking at the overall architecture required for the program, including such things as databases needed, hardware required, the language for programming and coding standards, and the IDE (Integrated Development Environment), a software application that provides

51

comprehensive facilities to help computer programmers such as a code editor, a debugger to find software errors, and ways to automate the programming.

Many programs, especially those meant to be used Enterprise–wide, include hundreds to thousands of pages of code. One of the first steps is laying out an overall initial design, which includes a list of the major tasks or functions which the program has to meet.

Our group met daily to lay out the total code design. This lasted for a period I am now estimating at approximately four to six months. (Yes, you read that correctly. That was four to six months before coders ever started to code.) The next chapter will look closely into this period with lots of detail.

The members of our group included a Business Analyst, a Requirements Lead, and a Technical Architect. Those who would do the actual coding were included. We also brought in a database administrator and a software testing individual. I began as the Requirements Lead and later moved to Project Management.

During the design phase, we concentrated on preparing a list of the major tasks, or functions, which the code would be asked to carry out. Once we had a list of these major tasks, we turned to the preparation of "use cases".

Use cases lay out, for each major task or function, every detail/outcome that can occur and how to deal with it when you are carrying out a task.

For example, if one is writing a program to handle purchases from a food truck, one major task will be to Purchase Food. Purchase Food will become one use case.

The use case details not only determining what food is purchased, but it will also detail what should happen if a customer decides **not** to purchase a food item that they have already picked up, or if they try to return an item or if their credit card is refused. This is all written in English but serves for the programmers as directions for coding. **Every single possible outcome** should be included for each use case.

The reason for use cases is that they direct what the programmers need to include in their code and **how to do so,** for example, how to handle that return. The use cases are extremely important, as you would want most of these decisions to made by those with a full understanding of the project in the real world. *(Good descriptions of how to write use cases are available on the web.)*

Following completion of the use cases, software designers also often include a series of activity diagrams which provide the same type of direction to the coders as the use cases. (In the early days, activity diagrams – called flowcharts – were included to provide final direction.)

Implementation. When the use cases and activity graphics are complete, they are given to the coders who actually do the coding. The coding can easily take four to six months.

When a section of coding is complete, it is then "unit tested", which involves putting together the pieces needed for that particular program component (the code, the database, etc.) to see if they work together and integrate with previous code.

Testing. When these code components are all completed and are found to work together well, they go through two more series of tests: system testing (tests the system as a whole and how it works) and acceptance testing (tests among the users to make sure the program is accomplishing what the users are looking for.)

Problem Areas

It is important to know that programs similar to Waterfall are in use in most computer science departments of any size. The program works well, or it would not be so widely used. However, there are some problems.

Remember we talked about the four to six months spent looking at the design of the program and writing use cases **before** we ever put pen to paper to do any coding.

If you have done your own coding, you know that once you have decided on an overall approach and you have laid out graphical charts, you may as well go right ahead to the code. It is already on the tip of your tongue. When you put four to six months in between "design" and "code", you will have a large block of time reconstructing where you were at end of your design phase. Net, net, my opinion — also called heresy — is that the Waterfall approach is significantly less than optimal in terms of time and more important, keeping pieces of the project integrated.

> **Problem: With months between original planning for use cases, etc., and the actual code generation, the Waterfall Method may end up adding coding time simply for refreshing memories of the original planning.**

One other problem actually lurks in the background. By the time the coding is ready for "acceptance" testing by the prospective users, it can be a year since the stakeholders have seen or heard anything about the program. The first issue is whether or not the issues are even relevant in the new time space.

> **With the Waterfall Method, stakeholders do not see any code until the whole program is finished. Since this period can be months long, one possible outcome is that the situation has changed for the stakeholders and there is now little interest in this particular program or in the way the program is handled.**

Chapter 7: Code Design for Object–Oriented Languages

Chapter Six presented code design for most, if not all, programming languages. The present chapter is going to examine code design further, but only for Object–Oriented Languages (OOP).

Almost all high level programming jobs will depend on OOP, as it is behind the three major languages used today; Java (and its variants J2EE and Java SE 6), VisualBasic.NET (and VB 6), and C (along with C# and C++) plus many others.

This is the type of programming that most of our country's IT departments depend on. Interestingly, from a programmer's point of view, the base object–oriented programming language (*the language itself*) is very much like its simpler variants from the 1970's and 1980's. However, where OOP differs in the *organization* of the code and that makes a big difference. We will look at the organization, so do not panic that there is more programming to come.

There is not more programming to come. We are just going to "do" organization. By organizing the code into a series of segments, we can exert control over what may become thousands of pages of code.

Functions and Subroutines

Early on in programming, frequently there were **operations that needed to be carried out more than once in a program** – operations such as calculating the tax on an item in a restaurant, converting euros to dollars at certain ATM's, determining interest paid, determining whether a particular wave is present in a brain scan, etc. It didn't make sense to write the same code more than once. Instead, subprograms called functions or subroutines were written to carry out these operations. (Functions produce one result; subroutines produce more than one.)

These segments of code were placed at or after the end of the program and when "called", the program would calculate what the function or subroutine specified and then transfer the answer back to the main program. Execution would resume on the line following the call in the main program.

However, functions could be troublesome. By declaring a variable as "global", in certain circumstances these functions could end up with access to (and the ability to change) variables from the main program. As a result, a lot of things could go wrong if numerous functions plus the main program *all* had the ability to change the value of a major variable in the program and the programmer didn't know when or how it was going to happen. It was more than difficult to uncover programming errors in these situations.

Object–Oriented Programming: A Solution To The Function Problem

Object–Oriented Programming was able to provide a solution to the problem. **The idea was to "encapsulate" the function, along with all the variables/data needed to carry out that function, into some kind of entity or object. This function would be called a Class.** In encapsulation the *variables* used in such a class are hidden from other parts of the program and can be used only within the current class. (Note: Not to worry. The machine and the language take care of all the details about finding a place to keep these class variables and managing communication between the class and the main program.)

To make it easier to think about such an object, think of an object named CheckingAccount. One function (a function is frequently also called an operation or a method) which might be a part of the object is — getEndingCheckingAccountTotal. The data/variables need to produce this operation would be customerAccountNumber, amountDeposited, amountWithdrawn, and beginningChecking Account Total.

When it comes time to use this function, the program will make available to the function the data needed to produce the desired output (customerAccountNumber, amountDeposited, amountWithdrawn, and beginningCheckingAccountTotal). The function will use this data to calculate the output of the function (getEndingCheckingAccountTotal). As you can see, everything needed to get the ending total is included in the object itself.

Object–Oriented programming occupies a major position within computing today. The major languages all have accommodated Object–Oriented programming in some manner.

Classes As Blueprints For Making Objects

Classes work in the following manner. When a call is made to a Class, an exact duplicate of the class is made – the duplicate is called an Object. The Object is used to carry out the function.

Look at it this way. Each time we make a new object it is like using a blueprint for a new house in a housing development. When we go to build the next house, we use the Class as a blueprint to make a new Object/the new house. Each new object is a completely different, separate entity. But each object has all the properties and functions of the original Class.

One way to look at this procedure is that OOP programming is simply a way of organizing code so pieces of code from different parts of the program cannot trip over one another. *The actual code in a function is not different from any code used to program in that language*

Needless to say OOP programming also solves another problem. Actually, object–oriented programming originally came about as a solution to the problem of many users deploying the same program at the same time. One version of a segment of code (the class) is kept to use as a blueprint. Then as each new user asking for a new Object comes along, a copy of that blueprint is produced (the object) for the new user to use. *This keeps multiple programmers from writing over each other's work.*

Problem Area: Object–Oriented Programming in the Real World: What Goes Wrong

What you don't know up to now is that object–oriented concepts have been found to be one of the most difficult concepts to get across — even to the brightest of students.

A university business school (with which I was familiar) had a required course in Java. Students taking the course just could not seem to grasp how to define the Classes and how to use them. And it is no wonder. If you take a good look at most texts for Java, for example, you will see that most of the texts **do not teach** one how to find or define a good Class. I had the privilege of taking the Oracle Training University authorized Java course. My course went on and on about classes but never mentioned how to define one or find one.

This whole situation always reminds me of the neighbor's kid who was summarily kicked out of grade school for his failure to know how to tie his shoes. No wonder: Mom had always dressed him in shoes with the hook and loop closures. Good for Mom.

Below are some thoughts from Microsoft on C++, another object–oriented language, about the introduction of Visual Basic.

In the early 1990s, it appeared that C++ was going to take the world by storm. This is because C++ permitted programmers to create classes that could be reused and extended by other programmers within the organization. In theory, this seemed like the silver bullet that corporate IS departments were looking for. To switch metaphors, this was the 'Holy Grail' of code reusability and the ability to not rewrite functionality from scratch for each project. However, in practice, things didn't quite work out this way. C++ classes are very abstract and difficult to use. And so programmers would change the classes for each project making reuse more of a dream than a reality.

https://msdn.microsoft.com/en–us/library/aa227231(v=vs.60).aspx

We'll see in a minute that defining classes or how to find classes is not a difficult task. *My experience, however, tells me that how to find classes is a topic that is just not taught.* Or, alternatively, it is not taught as a way of promoting code re–use and safe code organization. Let me tell you what I did see during my times as a project manager.

I did see extensive use of the OOP programming languages, Java/C/Visual Basic.Net. What I did not see is extensive use within the programs of organized lists of classes.

> **Problem: Actually, looking at the number of companies for whom I worked and the number of different projects on which I worked, it is surprising that I never saw an organized list of Classes for one of these programs. I also never saw a Class re–used. I never saw a Class diagram. My husband reports having had the same experiences.**

What I tended to see instead was a "linear" approach to the programs. The programs were written just like the old linear Fortran programs were written. Whenever a new function was needed, the coders just inserted a new Class.

Little Code Reuse Makes Errors Harder to Find

Even more important, when it comes to debugging (finding and correcting errors in a program), the less the reuse of classes, the greater the number of places the programmer has to go to "correct" the error. And when the programmer misses some code where errors lie, we tend to get updates followed by updates followed by updates. Unfortunately, this situation causes a lot of lost profit when it happens at our big global companies and it tends to occur with older/legacy code.

Before leaving this section, I want to pass along perhaps **the "cardinal" rule of computer science. That** rule states that items (code, as well as data) should appear once and only once. The reason is simple. When segments of code get repeated, things get messy when coding needs updating. You have to find all of the appearances in order to be sure each one gets updated/changed and that they all get updated exactly the same way. And when you get something as complicated as Microsoft Word, it is a real job to make sure you have found all the instances. Oh yes, and that could be why the first update doesn't always make it and we have to do it all over again. Does that sound familiar? Does that give you one reason why we have so many updates?

> **Problem: When coders make little if any use of code–reuse, the more difficult it is to find code to make upgrades when they are necessary. Sloppy code organization with little code re– use is at least part of the reason for too many glitches and so many updates.**

The real problem we seem to be having is that courses seem to tell one all about Classes but they never tell you how to get one.

> **Problem: Many courses in Object Oriented Languages do not teach you how to find or how to use a class.**

Alternative Solutions: You've Got to Be Carefully Taught.

The trick is the following: you have to get a book on "design" – "object–oriented design" — to get the info.

But nobody knows they need to go find that "design" book.

(Rowlett, T. W. (2000) The Object-Oriented Development Process. New Jersey: Prentice Hall.)

Pitifully, getting a well–organized set of Classes is easy. See below.

Most of the time, when coders are given an assignment for a software package, it will come with a **description of what is desired – a "vision" statement**. If you look closely at the vision statement, you will find that the **major nouns used in the statement will make pretty good classes.**

Below is a sample vision statement. It simply lays out in non–technical language what the program is expected to accomplish.

> *Katya and Marshall are opening their new food truck. They will be selling Tacos and Tostados for food and sodas or tea for drinks; Each customer first selects their purchases. The program then calculates the total purchase of food items and total drink items. Tax is added, 4% for food and 6% for drinks. At this point the customer is asked if they wish to be a part of the Truck's "Cash Back" program. If so, the customer provides their name and address. At the end of the season, a rebate will be sent to the customer of 2% on food items and 1% on drink items.*

One way of designing classes is to look at the major nouns used in the vision. A major noun listing would suggest that we could select classes from among these nouns: Purchases (consisting of/modified by tacoBuy, tostadaBuy, sodaBuy, teaBuy), Taxes (consisting of /modified by foodTaxes, drinkTaxes), Customer (modified by firstName, lastName), and Cashback (consisting of/modified by foodrebate, drinkrebate).

The main/non–modified nouns become the classes. The verbs become the functions (also called methods) used in each class. The adjectives or nouns that are modified by a noun (e.g., tacoBuy) become the attributes/variables/data.

In class modeling, each class is portrayed as a box, with the class name in the top box, the attributes/variables/data in the middle box and the functions/methods in the bottom box.

Classes "Purchases" and "Taxes"

Purchases	Taxes
tacoBuy tostadaBuy sodaBuy teaBuy	foodTaxes drinkTaxes
getFoodBuy getDrinksBuy	getFoodTaxes getDrinkTaxes

Classes "Customers" and "Cashback"

Customers	Cashback
firstName lastName	foodRebate drinkRebate
getFirstName getLastName	getfoodRebate getDrinkRebate

At this step, it is a good idea to go through the scenario once again, to make sure that the methods above will actually do all the calculations/operations that need to be carried out for Aunt Mary.

Note that for our Aunt Mary example, the computer program to be written will have a "main" program followed by four classes: Purchases, Taxes, Customers and Cashback. And in turn, the Purchases class will have all the code needed to work with purchases, i.e., determining exactly what is purchased. In particular, it will have the code to get the food bought and the code to get the drinks bought.

Problem Area: Why Object Oriented Programming Is So Vulnerable

The real question is why Object–Oriented Programming is so vulnerable. I am going to suggest that some of those teaching these types of courses may simply be teaching the way they were taught. (This is not everybody, but just some who did not get the training they needed in the design aspects of OOP.)

If the beginning professor had not been taught how to easily define Classes, and if that professor was heavily steeped in linear Fortran, a linear approach may be what surfaces when the beginning professor teaches. Keep in mind that many professors have spent most of their professional life in a linearly–oriented world. Maybe it is just too easy to drop back into linearly–oriented programming. Note that this approach can then transfer itself all the way down the system.

> **Problem: One of the biggest problems may be that we don't have enough teachers well trained in how to teach the object–oriented languages and we do not have enough who understand the implications of OOP and design in a large scale production environment.**

When you are observing events and when you are not in a position to set up experimental methods to determine what is going on, you are left with estimations of what may be the case. I can't prove that this is what may be happening, although in a number of conversations with those teaching OOP, their roots in the older style of linear programming surface quickly.

One instance which helped lead me to the above hypothesis happened during the middle of a design session after we had just defined the Use Cases. I suggested we go on at that point to define the Classes. (Note: I was not the project lead for this part of the coding.) The coders responded with one very consistent blank stare. They literally did not know what I was talking about. O.K. I am so proud to tell you that after a couple of days of verbal wrestling, I backed off the subject. We never did set up a Class diagram.

The coders were using one of the popular IDE's, Integrated Development Environments. As we noted before,

IDEs are an application in which almost all development is done. This application typically provides many features which will help the coder when authoring, modifying, compiling, deploying and finding coding error in the software.

> **Problem: Some popular IDE's (Integrated Development Environments) are Eclipse, Microsoft Visual Studio, WebSphere, and Rational XDE. These IDE's will take you step by step through setting up an entire outline for a Class. My coders were way along in the coding before they ever used these outlines. And their Classes were designed in a very much linear fashion – every time they needed a particular function, they just defined another Class (i.e. selected a new outline) and used the new outline.**

Alternative Solutions: Better Teaching

Solutions to the above problems are fairly easy and have been covered before. First, we need to ensure that our professors and teachers are well versed in and teaching the "design" part of Object–Oriented Programming. Confusion over OOP will continue so long as students are not taught how to go about defining classes. When they are taught how to define them, it makes sense that OOP is simply a formal method of code re–use and code organization.

Second, we need to make sure that the following idea is the norm rather than the exception. We want to get away from the linear form of programming and realize the virtue of only coding segments of code once and let the program re–use that code when appropriate. When code only occurs once, it is easy to find and easy to correct if needed. If the same code appears numerous times, it is first necessary to make sure all appearances are caught and second to make sure all appearances contain the same code and are not coded differently. If they are coded differently, especially if mathematical equations are present, one can get different answers, if only in the last few decimal points.

Chapter 8: IT Departments: A View from the Inside

Chapters Two and Three began by introducing and showing what programming really is. Chapter Four looked at learning one's first programming language. Chapter Five moved from there to getting that first programming job. Things got quite a bit more skilled when Chapters Six and Seven moved directly into Code Design.

Now I would like to move to what actually happens inside one of the typical larger IT departments. This section will, by rights, be somewhat more on the personal side. And of course I will lay out problem areas which tend to occur in these departments.

Before going into the course of programming for a project, I need to lay out the organization and environment in which the coding will occur. This will provide you with some understanding of how varied these departments can be and how varied some of the jobs can be.

You may quietly be wondering what the organizational structure of a department or even the physical structure may have to do with producing excellent code. This section in reality is all about how one reacts to their working environment. What it really has to do with is how that environment makes you feel as a worker. Are you needed? Are you appreciated? Do you feel as if you are really making a contribution? Or alternatively do you feel as if you are just a number, with little value to the firm?

Background: Department Organization

Note: For the rest of the book, I will be describing situations that occurred at places where I worked. I will also be including, every so often, situations described to me by close friends, i.e., by those I can count on to describe things accurately.

From 1998 until I retired in 2008, I had a career in IT. Over that ten–year time period, I was a contract employee at four different firms. Three of the firms for which I worked were the traditional IT contracting firms. The remaining one was a generalized staffing firm that provided temps for all areas of work, but much of the work I did for them ended up to be IT–related.

From those four contracting firms I was contracted out to four different corporations: two Fortune 500 firms, one which would later become a part of a Fortune 500 firm and one which would later become a part of a Forbes Global 2000 firm.

What I would like to do in this section is describe what my placements were like. Over the four they were very, very different.

Different Types of Departments

Placement in an IT Department. Of the four firms, for 2 of those I was hired directly into the IT department. The two IT departments both had, I'm estimating, between

50 and 100 employees each. Our bosses had high level programming and IT skills.

Looking at the IT departments, the main work I did was connected to the design of software applications. I was a Requirements Lead for both firms. (My main responsibility was collecting requirements for a new application such as the number of expected users.) Later, for one firm I became the Project Manager for that application. (I was responsible for the output of 23 programmers and other IT types.) Project Manager and Requirements Lead are two of the software design types that the U.S. Labor Department notes are in great need.

Placement in Business/Marketing Area. For the remaining two firms, I was hired into the general business/marketing area. Neither firm had more than four employees in our group. Our direct bosses in the marketing and business areas were *not* generally IT knowledgeable.

For those placements reporting into marketing and general business, (and also for a while in one of the IT departments) I was involved primarily with accessing data from large databases. In order to get at very large and complex databases and for pure efficiency, we used Access (a single user database program, part of Microsoft Office) and, for one project, SPSS (a major statistical system that includes database access features.

These two job descriptions may tell you the importance of getting data in and out of databases. Much of that is for marketing purposes. We frequently were involved in making up mailing lists for major advertising campaigns.

You may find it interesting that Access jobs are considered at the low end of IT employment. Project management is considered at the high end. Project Management will usually attract the higher salary.

The bosses. At the IT departments, the bosses did have advanced IT and programming skills. At one we were regularly sent out for training. I had training in Java from an Oracle Training University and in Project Management from Gopal Kapur at the Center for Project Management. *(This was an arrangement not to last long. The CEO was let go before we could say thank you.)*

> **Problem: Too few IT employers regularly send their personnel out for advanced training. Because languages and applications change so frequently in IT, this situation can easily lead to "holes" in training, for example, the person understands the newer security features but not database features.**

Problem Area: Adding Code from the Outside.

Note also here that when I was working in the marketing departments, the marketing bosses were not knowledgeable in the languages and apps we were using. What that meant was that the only person watching over the code was the top coder. Coders could add code from outside sources or from the internet. The boss would not be aware of the addition.

The situation inside the marketing departments, however, may not be as harmful as in **the IT departments (with code savvy bosses)** where the programmers tend to pick up and include code from the same or a different language from outside sources or off the internet for short sequences.

Often the change is being made to make it easier to design forms for web sites or to make it easier to do database accesses or for some other reason.

It is not difficult to pick up code off the internet. Several examples can be available if one Googles the topic one needs. These examples often provide actual code ready to go. The coder only needs to highlight the code desired. To highlight, position the mouse over the first word of the section desired. Then, holding down the left mouse button, move the mouse across the total desired code. Once highlighted, press the "Control" key. While continuing to hold down the Control key, press C at the same time. Move the mouse to where you would like a copy and press CTRL simultaneously with V.

The problem arises when it is not clear to all involved and not documented that a change has been made. **The situation becomes particularly troublesome when updates to the program are being made and no one even knows an extra language is there.**

Now, there are times when a language which is particularly good for a specific purpose, such as character recognition, will be selected for certain segments of a larger program will full knowledge of all involved. This type of action normally causes no problems because it is well documented and not a surprise. On the other hand, I've been warned by a colleague that one still has to watch out that the picked up code does not contain *more instructions than planned on, making it unclear exactly what the code is going to produce.*

> **Problem: Because managers of IT areas do not always possess IT skills, programmers can code in languages not expected or in open source/free languages and the managers are not always aware this is going on. Languages can be added *even* in IT departments with code knowledgeable bosses simply because often the only persons to examine the code are the coding team.**

The real problems come when data updates need to be done. We can guess that some part of the time the current programmers will not be as facile in the particular open source languages/apps as the original coders. Even more frightening, they may simply not be aware of its presence. This is not hard when programs get as big as many do. (Typical large programs can often be as large as a couple thousand pages.) That's where mistakes get made. The documentation for the software will also tend not to be correct.

> **Problem: Software tends to become unmanageable when coders are using open source software (free to everyone) from the outside and not all are aware of and/or competent in the materials being used.**

Alternative Solution: The Code Reviewer

One possible suggestion for larger firms to address the problem of "unknown software" was first talked about in the chapter on "too many languages." That suggestion was the addition of a "software expert" or "software reviewer".

Middle to larger firms may wish to consider the addition of a "software reviewer". This person would have a position outside any of the coding groups. Their job would be to look over everybody's software at various times during development. Their tasks would include uncovering too little code re–use or too much use of open source that isn't documented.

Background: The Environment

For two firms I had a nice, full–sized cubicle. One was an IT department; the other was a general business/marketing department. (Before you get positive, however, compare that to a corner office on the 22nd floor of a glass high–rise during my advertising career. My how times changed over the years.) For the two firms with a nice–sized cubicle, the surroundings were either brand new or not too old and in good shape.

Problem Area: The Environment

For the remaining two, I shared a cubicle with another person – again, one IT department and one business/marketing department. One cubicle was approximately 5' by 5'. The second was 5' by 7'. For both, one person had to pull their chair in toward the desk before the second person could get out of the cubicle. *(This movement did require substantial leg unfolding, which tended to remind some of us of a not–so–elegant Argentine Tango.)* Further note: This arrangement did not leave one with a real positive view of their job position.

For one firm with the small cubicles, I shared my cubicle (at different times) with three other persons. When you are this close to someone, they had better be nice to be around. All three of my cubby–mates were, thank goodness.

However, for the two firms with small cubicles, my first reaction to the work surroundings was to make an emergency call to Merry Maids, Stanley Steamer, and Scrubbing Bubbles all at once. At one of these two firms, when we were moved to a new work area, you should have seen each of us on day 2: A Giant Bounty in one hand and a Giant Windex in the other, standing on a table, washing windows and the Venetian blinds.

The story at the second firm was that the employees (not the contract workers – the real employees) had written a formal request to the CEO to ask to have the carpets cleaned. The answer coming back was that if the employees wanted cleaner carpets they should clean them themselves. And every other Friday the guy six cubicles over rolled in his Bissell cleaner and washed the carpet in *his* cubicle.

> **Problem: Productivity may suffer due to employee surroundings at some organizations. Perhaps a little less emphasis on quarter to quarter profits and more emphasis on employee surroundings might provide positive incentives.**

Alternative Solution: The Importance of Cleanliness

Actually, the H–1B's were a little embarrassed to show us pictures of their offices in India. They were beautiful, brand new, high rise buildings with activity centers, day–care centers, cafeterias, etc. The outside of the buildings I saw and the campus looked like some of the Silicon Valley businesses.

I don't think U.S. workers always expect brand new buildings. Many of our businesses tend to be older, and some are very nice. However, cleanliness certainly has its virtues and should be considered.

81

Background: Changes Over Time

The early part of my IT career — around the turn of the century. Previously my discourse moved back and forth between IT departments and business/marketing departments. Hopefully, it did not drive you nuts. The purpose was to help disguise the particular firms to which comments belonged, especially in cases where my comments were not positive. Now let's turn to how we were treated as employees. The main differentiator here is time. We'll be comparing early on to later on in my ten years in IT.

At first we contract personnel were treated very much like real employees. We were invited to business meetings of the firm, to their parties, such as the Holiday Dinner Dance, to charity and other firm affairs, like hot dog day. Not only that, our contracting firm was ever so good to us. My first birthday brought the world's most incredulous chocolate cake with icing three inches high. Regularly we were taken to lunch by someone from the contracting firm just to check out how well we liked our assignment. If we had a problem, we could be moved to another placement quickly. (And I was on one occasion.)

However, as rumor had it, Microsoft and others in Silicon Valley (and I'm sure some firms elsewhere) were replacing too many employees with contract players and not giving the contract personnel a number of benefits. A number of lawsuits plus some directives coming out of the Department of Labor led to a set of rules for the handling of contract — contingent personnel.

Problem Area

Later on. Toward the end of my contracting work, a lot of emphasis was placed on making sure we were *not* treated as employees. We were never invited to any business meetings of the firm. (Rule #1 for non–competitiveness: Make sure your workers don't understand where the firm is going or what is important.) At company events, we were not to have our lunches or dinners paid for (an only partially successful directive). And most important, in those days for many of us, we could only work for 2 years straight at one firm. Now you understand why I was continually unemployed.

> **Problem: Due to Department of Labor recommendations and lawsuit outcomes, many companies allowed contract workers to only work for a firm for two years without making them employees. This directive represented a good opportunity for firms to lose expertise.**

Alternative Solution:

There is no pat, quick answer to this problem area. There need to be discussions (and a lot of them) about how the contract worker relates to the firm. We will only convince more kids to go into computer science if that occupation/career is considered a rewarding one.

Chapter 9: Enterprise Coding

In the last section we looked at the organization and physical set–up for the IT and marketing departments in which I worked or ones of which I was aware. We did not look at the personnel in those departments, how they worked together, and how they designed and coded the software. Let us take a closer look at one IT department which was and is pretty typical of 21st century departments. At the time, this department was set up to write a J2EE enterprise application to be used worldwide. Also a part of the project was an H–1B firm from India along with its personnel.

Background

Before I start this section, I would like to make a few comments about the team involved with this project. This is particularly necessary because I am going to make some less than favorable comments about things I saw and heard — all for the purpose of helping us improve our software outputs.

This team had some of the brightest and most professional workers I have seen. Given that working conditions were not always the best, they still came to work every day with an attitude that they would give their best. If work required more hours, they were there. If corrections needed to be made, they were there. When an application or language was added, it was because it was going to improve their output. I will argue that their short–term improvement may not always have made for long–term improvement, but that is not the issue. At the time, their additions were an improvement.

The most skilled member of the department was a software developer (that's the next step up from a coder/programmer) with a recent degree in computer science from a large and prestigious American research university. He had a broad background in computer science. He was highly skilled in several major languages and probably one of the brighter individuals I have met. His main activity was to lead a lot of the design and coding. (The organization was absolutely flat. We were all among a group of over 60 employees reporting on the same level to the same boss.)

The firm had formed a group of graduates who had been hired at the same time as our lead programmer above. They let these programmers know that they were considered to be among the best and that the firm was there to help and would do everything they could to make sure this working experience was useful and pleasant. In our group there were also two to three additional programmer employees whose skills I'm guessing were average to above average.

Also in the group was a lead software developer from the H–1B firm. In my experience his skill level was the equal of his American counterpart. His job was to coordinate activities with a group of around 9 to 12 programmers remaining in India. As such, his activities were half coder and half project manager for the coders in India.

The group of programmers remaining in India were, in my experience, very much on the beginning side. To give you a better idea, this group would have the skills that one might have after attending, say, a two–day class in learning Java with a couple of months of practice beyond that. It was clear from the beginning that one missing skill was writing using the Java language coding standards. *(The Java coding standards provide directions for punctuation, capitalization, and indentation when writing Java code. It is useful to note here that Java, with all its punctuation, gets very confusing and hard to follow if the coding standards are not strictly followed. It was also clear that most of the organization of the code was set up on the U.S. side and then provided to the coders in India.)*

Beyond the coders were a series of especially skilled, computing science personnel. Included were:

• **The Head Software Architect:** the software expert whose job it was to make the high–level design choices and dictate technical standards, including software coding standards, hardware and databases.

• **The Database Administrator:** the DBA — designer and maintainer of the major database used for the application. Works with a special application to aid in the design and maintenance. (A top flight DBA can add immeasurably to an application.)

• **The Main Tester(s):** responsible for assuring that the various components of the application work as specified (called unit testing), responsible for testing among users (acceptance testing), and responsible for all other testing of the application. Two filled the role over time here.

• **The Requirements Lead:** responsible for collecting requirements for the project, such as number of expected users and for seeing to it that they were being followed.

• **The Business Analyst:** responsible for coordinating with management and personnel to identify, define and document business needs and objectives.

• **The Project Manager:** responsible for the output of the group, its timing and its accuracy. I was the Project Manager. (I moved into the role when the first project manager left.)

Of interest, the main testers were H–1B's assigned to the U.S. The Head Architect, DBA, Business Manager, and Requirements Lead were U.S. employees. The Project Manager – me – was a contract worker. Of interest, one of the U.S. employees lived in another city and worked exclusively by phone and online.

The H–1B programmers were male. One tester was male and one was female. Of the U.S. employees, half were male and half were female. Remember that these were high level employees. Note that half of these "software engineers" were female.

Time sheets and budgeting required my inputting salary figures. A set of figures was provided — one for each of the salary ranges — to use for the time sheets. These figures provided some sort of average salary but kept the real figures confidential. The U.S. employees were entered with a salary approximately 60% greater than the one entered for the H–1B workers and the American contract worker. Figures for the coders in India were not available.

While H–1B workers should be paid the same as U.S. employees with those skills, one could argue that, having not worked for the firm before, the salaries of these H–1B employees would be at the entry level of the salary range for that job title. **Actually, a 2011 report from the National Accounting Office found that half of all H–1Bs were brought in at entry–level wages.**

(http://www.nytimes.com/2013/04/12/technology/tech-firms-push-to-hire-more-workers-from-abroad.html).

Given the salary range with which I was working, it is apparent that the H–1Bs were being paid for skills at the entry level. It is difficult to argue that these were "highly skilled" personnel that were hired because U.S. computer science personnel who were highly skilled could not be found.

Perhaps you also have the question of whether American jobs were being replaced by the H–1B's. All I can tell you is that for a few weeks after I joined the project, I would see an H–1B arrive. Then I would see a U.S. employee leave. It happened two to three times in our project.

The H–1B and other contract firms were paid typically twice each personnel's salary. Half was salary and half was overhead. There would also have been overhead for the firm's employees, but I did not know what that figure was.

Following Activities for a Major Application

The section below follows the activities of the group for an enterprise–wide application for which I was the Project Manager.

The department followed the full life cycle development model for the design and development of software. The specific model used was Waterfall. Its principles involve a sequential design where each design phase has to be completed before the next phase is started. The phases we used were: requirements, design, development, testing, and implementation.

During the first couple of phases, all the members of the group listed above met daily to lay out the requirements and overall design. This lasted for a period I am now estimating at approximately four to six months. The team completed the design through writing the use cases and producing activity diagrams. A graphical version of the use cases (which I noted before, for those of you with IT backgrounds, comes very close to the flowcharts used early on in computing.)

Problem Areas

I would like to include some observations, but I should caution that, in my mind, one key characteristic of IT employees (plus a lot of other types of employees today) is their ability to keep a great deal secret. One way to keep your job safe is to only let your colleagues know what is absolutely necessary. Now, keeping information to oneself does not enhance the development process, especially in the early phases of development. This propensity for secrecy does make things harder for a writer like me, but I can tell you a lot from just observation.

The first round of actual code writing was done in India. The coders were given the use case and the graphics. They would produce a first code draft under close supervision. Then that draft went to the H–1B programmer in the U.S. He would refine the code. Then the code would go to the lead U.S programmer and the code would be refined ever further. This method seems to be a bit of an overkill, or alternatively, not the height of efficiency.

At the beginning of the coding, emails were indicating that much of the work was simply rewriting to meet Java coding standards. We haven't talked a lot about coding standards until now. There exists a set of standards for writing code in Java. They consist of punctuation, capitalization, indenting, etc., all of which makes the code easier to read and easier to immediately recognize as Java.

> **Problem: At the beginning, code that is outsourced may need to be re–written simply to conform to Java coding standards.**

The other part of the observation is that the initial code was substantially and repeatedly re-done before it reached those with the authority to approve a code module. The time taken here was way beyond that needed for meeting coding standards. The question is whether a certain salary must be paid before outsourcing a job becomes worth the investment.

> **Problem: Outsourced coding may need to be substantially re–written beyond just for coding standards. This will affect final costs and budgeting.**

Even now, I would like to know how many stakeholders (those who are actually going to use the software) feel that they are having enough of an opportunity for input while the code is being developed. While we would call a stakeholder when there was a question, I'm not sure it was frequent enough. It certainly was not frequent enough for the stakeholder to feel as if they were a real part of the design.

> **Problem: On too many occasions, stakeholders for larger projects may feel that their input is less than optimal.**

Another possible problem is one that I just happened to come across while looking down on a desk. One of the team members had been given the task of using WebSphere, our development environment, to produce outlines for some segment of the code. The job did not get done and did not get done. I think that eventually what happened was that the lead programmer took over the task and it got done. I concluded that this was an indication that even with such a large team, we still only had one person who was fully skilled in the basic developmental environment for our application.

> **Problem: While using IDE's (Integrated Developmental Environments) will ease the coding, many are quite sophisticated applications. There may be a need to make sure team members are skilled in the best use of the IDE. Extra training may be needed. These applications are not always easy to use to their fullest.**

One note is necessary here. The chapter on Object–Oriented Design hopefully goes a long way to make classes easier to understand. However, there are a lot of different ways to define features of the classes that I never even mentioned. These features provide a lot of flexibility for the software developer. However, many of these are quite high level and take a substantial amount of experience to understand and use well. The IDE's help define these features, but one has to understand them before one starts.

Problems: Additional Areas

Regardless of what one is doing, there is always the person who wants to make a change. Even more often, changes need to be made because of something that somebody forget or something that currently is wrong. You will hear a lot about projects that get totally slowed down due to change orders.

I have to be honest. I did not have problems with change orders. Of course, where I was we required that change orders be signed by a Vice President. Getting that signature was brutal. Not only that, for a period of time after the signature, the Project Manager had to be available for questioning once a week. Again, brutal.

> **Change orders may be a cause of slowdown in many projects. Some firms make it very difficult to get a change order. On the other hand, some very good firms make sure that when change is needed, it goes through easily. Change orders require balance.**

Unit testing is really important to the success of the application. Unit testing is done following coding to ensure that the components of the program work together in the specified manner, Acceptance testing occurs after all the coding is complete and is carried out to see that the program is acceptable to the users. In both cases, the program is run — usually with some sample data — to see how well the program performs.

However, I have now heard from several different sources that a frequent problem with the unit testing is that the testing folks consider a piece of software to pass the unit test if the software "compiles", that is, if it "runs" without stopping due to errors. It does not have to get the right answer.

Back in our Fortran example, if I change one of the examples from (Midtrm1 + Midtrm2 + Midtrm3)/3.0 to Midtrm1 + Midtrm2 + Midtrm3/3.0, the software will run but the answer will be wrong. We had that problem with the testers but caught it quickly.

> **Problem: It is critical to check unit testing to make sure that it is testing whether the correct answer has been delivered. Checking to see that the code "runs" is not sufficient. New applications must get correct answers.**

Now that we've finished with numerous criticisms, it is helpful to mention that the department above may well have been one of the better departments around. Try this next example department on for size. In this department, the main activity was calculating the daily inventory of stock. There was a nice application in Access. The only problem was that no one, and I seriously mean no one, knew what the formulas were for calculating that inventory. The stakeholders frequently wanted changes but somehow did not realize that coders really couldn't do that without knowing the formulas. (I used to keep a genie under my desk for situations like this, but he just never would come out of that bottle and give me the formulas.) Some of you are wondering why reverse engineering was not tried. It was. The program was simply too complicated. Let me end by saying that accurately documenting what has been programmed is a pretty good first step toward IT excellence.

Problem: What I want to emphasize is the idea that for the first round, some of these problems might not seem so serious. However, when one is on the fifteenth update, the sloppier the organization of the code, the more inefficient the design, and the weaker the documentation of the code, the more difficult it is going to be to accurately make changes.

Alternative Solutions

Looking back at the problem areas above, many, if not most of them, are day–to–day happenings. The solution to them is simply to keep a watchful eye out for any activities which will inhibit the output of excellent code and to turn them around, on the spot.

Chapter 10: Agile — A Better Way to Develop Software

Up to this point we have been pretty brutal in addressing the foibles of the Waterfall Full Life Cycle Development procedure. Perhaps it would be a good idea to point out that Waterfall is currently directing software in departments and firms across the world. Waterfall has faults, but almost any procedure is going to have faults.

On the other hand, there is a procedure that I have used and that I really like. It's called **Agile**. Its chief characteristics are early and continuous delivery of software. It is done by taking even the largest potential software package and breaking it into small increments — increments that can be finished in, say, one to four weeks.

Each iteration involves a cross–functional team working on all the following functions: planning, requirements analysis, design, coding, unit testing, and acceptance testing. At the end of the iteration a working product is demonstrated to stakeholders.

99

One absolute key to the success of Agile is the one that may be hardest to accomplish. Agile asks that every team includes at least one customer representative. The customer representative will be there to oversee each increment to make sure it is meeting customer needs. I had questioned earlier whether the Waterfall method lent itself to frequent enough interaction with the business group. On the large project talked about in Chapter 5, only one member of the team talked to the business group.

Agile development methodology provides opportunities to assess and/or change the direction of a project throughout the development lifecycle. This is achieved through regular increments of work, known as sprints or iterations. At the end of each iteration, the team must present a potentially shippable product increment.

In waterfall, development teams only have one chance to get each aspect of a project right. In an Agile paradigm, every aspect of development — requirements, design, etc. — is continually revisited throughout the lifecycle. When a team stops and re–evaluates the direction of a project every few weeks, course correction is fairly easy.

Agile design helps avoid a frequent problem. When I have talked to others, I have found something I would not expect. That is the case where the computer science team works on a very large project for, say, six months to a year. Check later and you will find that somewhere along the line the project just got dropped after its completion. It is not being used at all.

I am going to take a guess that when the software finally got over to the business group, the group found some major part missing. I am also guessing that they would also figure that it would be another six months or so to get the missing part completed and that there are enough other little things they would like that might take even more time. So the project just gets dropped. However, when developing with Agile, the business group is there all the time. They will catch and change the parts they don't like or the parts that are missing.

A common characteristic of Agile is the daily "stand–up", also known as the daily scrum. In a brief session, team members report to each other what they did the previous day toward their team's sprint goal, what they intend to do today toward their team's sprint goal, and any roadblocks or impediments they can see to their team's sprint goal. The rule for the daily scrum is that everyone stands – no sitting. That ensures that the meeting won't last too long.

Of interest, when I was working with a Waterfall project I had instituted a temporary daily meeting to make sure we were on track after we missed one of the deadlines. After about two weeks, I told the group that we really didn't have to continue having this daily meeting. All of a sudden there was a definite roar over the phone lines with everyone yelling, "Oh yes we do. Please don't cancel the meeting."

At that point I remembered what had always bugged me about work teams. It always seemed that there was some information that never got passed to all team members. In fact, the absolute strongest way personnel had and have of maintaining control was to maintain control over the passage of information. It was always worse if there was a small group who wanted to maintain control. They told each member everything and told me nothing.

I assured everyone that our "daily scrum" would continue. We did have one small change. Half of our group was in India, and one was in a Midwestern city. It seemed a little ridiculous to ask these guys to stand holding their phones, so this requirement was eased for those not in the office.

Agile has so many positives. The biggest one, of course, is the presence of continuing, completed software. The business group/stakeholders know that progress is being made and they know it fits their needs. They see the work that has been done. Contrast that to the Waterfall method where months pass by and the stakeholders see nothing done. That is why, if you ask them how good the computer group is, they may say they are a bunch who do little work. I was at the blunt end of one of these conversations. We had gone to extraordinary means to get things done on time and get them correct. We had literally turned around our output. But when management asked the stakeholders how we were doing, we got trashed.

On the opposite end, one of my most gratifying projects was when two of us were given three weeks to completely re–write the salary adjustments software for the company. We used Agile. The Human Resources second in command made himself totally available about half time. He sat behind us and several times noted that what we were doing couldn't be right because "so and so" should have had a different raise. As we would get each part/increment finished, he was there to say it was fine, just fine. Everyone was most pleased at the completion – on time, on budget, and correct.

Now for the most embarrassing project. This one occurred when I handed the finished software over to the stakeholders and they came back the next day to tell me that "the thing wouldn't even open." You really look good on that one. What I had done was to open the program with the date. But instead of putting the date in a "date" variable, I had put it in a text variable. The program didn't mind my variable because it took the form of a "date" and used it for the form of the text. However, my client used a different form of "date" and that type did not work. Had we been using Agile, that mistake would have been caught.

There is one possible negative to Agile development. Things occur so fast that often the project is completed before any documentation has even begun. The most common recommendation for documenting is to do as little as possible at first and fill out as necessary later. In other words, do not start with the assumption that you are going to write full documentation.

> **One present weakness of Agile Development is that it tends to provide documentation that might be described as the "bare**

> **minimum". It may be filled out further later on, if desired.**

There are many ways to do documentation. The one important part is just doing it, period.

Other arguments aside, the fact that Agile makes secrecy difficult is a strong positive in my estimation.

There is one final weakness having to do with Agile's main strength. One can question whether Agile has the ability to take on **very large**, Enterprise–wide projects. Agile may possibly get too many parts/increments or get parts cut up so small that it is easy to lose where one is going. On the other hand, there is no reason why there cannot be a nice halfway point between Waterfall and Agile where much larger pieces of the project area separated and **then** broken up into the increment parts.

> **By melding parts of the Waterfall design with parts of Agile, it may be possible for Agile to produce quite fine results, even with very large, Enterprise–wide projects.**

Chapter 11: Databases to Store your Data

I was somewhat surprised when I examined my IT placements and discovered that half of them involved pulling data from very large databases. *(Yes, Mom, data pulls can be a full–time job)*. I tend to think of myself on the programming/software development side. It just hadn't dawned on me how much of my income was dependent on database skills. This may tell you very quickly how important those databases are.

Think for a minute of Amazon having to store the charges and payments of their millions of customers across the globe. Think of Zillow keeping track of the latest sales price of their millions of listed homes across the country. And on the other end think of the local stamp club keeping a database of their members or a small dry cleaning business keeping a database of its customers. And it goes on and on.

Background: Retrieving Data Made Easy

A second clue to the importance of the database is the fact that a number of programs and frameworks have been written specifically to make it easier to retrieve data from bases:

- The basic language for virtually all large databases is SQL, the program designed specifically to develop databases and then to retrieve the data from those databases. Below are examples of four of its most used forms, all pulling from a table named CITIES with four columns: ID, City State, and SUMTEMP:

1. SELECT * FROM CITIES

   (* means select all columns)

2. SELECT * FROM CITIES WHERE

   SUMTEMP > 30.0

3. SELECT ID, CITY, STATE FROM CITIES

4. SELECT ID, CITY, STATE FROM CITIES

   WHERE SUMTEMP > 30.0

The basic language looks easy. But it is only fair to warn you that the SQL statements can become complicated very quickly, especially if there are a lot of restrictions, like age, sex, state, etc.

• Access is the Microsoft Office application to develop and manage databases. The most wonderful part about Access is a graphical data window in the program which allows one to pull data that you want into the window. At the same time, it actually writes the SQL statement for you.

• SPSS has an outline which also makes accessing data very easy.

Cardinal Rule

When we first started working with databases, we just added data on the end of the row when we needed more variables. (For example if we needed four customers for a sales person instead of three.) However, this approach had several basic drawbacks, the major of which was that it was really inefficient when it came to memory room. In addition, if you needed to add data on the end of one major table, you would also tend to find that you needed to make changes to tons of other tables. The solution to this problem was to *Normalize* a database. Virtually all big firm bases will tend to be normalized these days.

Before moving to directions on how to Normalize, I want to repeat **the "cardinal" rule of computer science. That rule states that items (*data, as well as code*) should appear once and only once.** The reason is simple. When segments of code get repeated, things get messy when coding needs updating. You have to find all of the appearances in order to be sure each one gets updated/changed and that they all get updated exactly the same way. And when you get something complicated, it is a real job to make sure you have found all the instances. Oh yes, and that could be why the first update doesn't always make it and we have to do it all over again. Does that sound familiar? Does that give you one reason why we have so many updates?

The same basic idea holds for data in databases. Each data piece should appear once and only once in a database. Otherwise, if that data piece is incorrect, you will have to find all instances of that data to correct. If George's birthdate is in only once and it is listed as 1984, when it should be 1985, you only have one correction to make. On the other hand, if the 1984 appears in several of the tables of the database, you will have a real job ahead of you to find all the incorrect instances and to make sure they are get corrected the same way.

Below is the sophisticated IT way of keeping the "only appears once" rule for the data side. It occurs by "Normalizing" a database.

Old Fashioned Database

Employee ID	Sales Person	Sales Office	Cust. Name	Cust. Name	Cust. Name
003	Holmes	Atlanta	Dell	Lenovo	
004	Chin	Miami	Acer	Lenovo	Apple
005	Doyle	Boston	Sony		

Above is how long ago we would have set up the Sales Staff Database for a graphics card supplier to computer makers. Note that Holmes' job is to sell graphics cards to two pc makers, Dell and Lenovo.

Normalizing Databases

But what happens to the database if Chin acquires a fourth customer? In the olden days, that often meant a rewrite of not one, but many tables in the database. Normalizing a database avoids problems like the one above.

Normalizing involves putting the data above through a series of transformations: First, Second, and Third Normal Forms. I'll show an example but use more everyday language to describe what happens.

What these changes do is 1) make the database as small and efficient as possible and 2) make is more difficult to introduce errors into the base. Below takes the table above and moves it through the three Normal forms.

Note: This section is difficult — even for a lot of us with a lot of experience. Feel free to skip the rest of this chapter if you wish.

First Normal Form:

Eliminate repeating groups in individual tables.

(The Customer name in the original table repeats in three columns, now down to one column)

Cust.ID	Employee ID	Cust. Name	Cust. City	Postal Code
1001	003	Dell	Denver	30303
1002	003	Lenovo	Seattle	89741
1003	004	Acer	Austin	65012
1004	004	Lenovo	Miami	88056
1005	004	Apple	Cupertino	95014
1006	005	Sony	Chicago	60601

…..

Employee ID	Sales Person	Sales Office
003	Holmes	Atlanta
004	Chin	Miami
005	Doyle	Boston

Second Normal Form:

Eliminate Redundant Data

Looking at 1st Normal Base, Sales Person 003 repeats in first 2 **rows**. Sales Person 004 repeats in next 3 **rows.**

Create a separate table for each set of related data

(Put Sales Person and Sales Office in one table because they are clearly related to each other.

.....

Customer ID	Customer Name	Customer City	Postal Code
1001	Dell	Denver	30303
1002	Lenovo	Seattle	89741
1003	Acer	Austin	65012
1004	Lenovo	Atlanta	88056
1005	Apple	Cupertino	95014
1006	Sony	Chicago	60601

.....

Employee ID	Sales Person	Sales Office
003	Holmes	Atlanta
004	Chin	Miami
005	Doyle	Boston

.....

Third Normal Form:

Identify each row with a unique column or set of columns (called the primary key). All columns in that table must be dependent on the primary key.

Eliminate data not dependent on the key and only the key.

One of the changes the Third Normal Form makes is to add a "key" (an I.D. number) and then define a new table which does *not* contain "related" data, that is, data in which one variable can be defined once you know the other.

Let me give you three examples. Remember that you are going for the most efficient base that is possible. First, you would not want to put car manufacturer in the same table as car model because once you know the model, you know the manufacturer, i.e., they are related. One is dependent on the other in the sense that a Forester will not become a Cadillac tomorrow. It just won't happen. In this case, it is best to keep the model and **remove the manufacturer** altogether from the base. You can always go to a source outside the base to find the manufacturer once you know the model.)

Second, you also wouldn't want to put a zip code in the same table as the city name. Zip code 63104 is in St. Louis. Tomorrow that zip code is not going to change to Atlanta. This just won't happen. However, the situation is a little more complicated because there are some zip codes that cover more than one city. Therefore, if you remove city totally from the base, you can't be absolutely sure that you know the city once you know the zip. One way to handle this is to **remove the city from the zip code table. Then, create a new table, Postal Code, which includes Postal Code as the primary key and City as its sole column.**

In the last example, Sales Person and Sales Office are not dependent on each other. While Holmes is in Atlanta today, there is nothing to stop Holmes from moving to Miami tomorrow. **Both columns stay in the base** because they are not related/not inherently dependent on each other.

http://www.essentialsql.com/get-ready-to-learn-sql-11-database-third-normal-form-explained-in-simple-english/

.....Customer ID	Customer Name	Customer Postal Code
1001	Dell	30303
1002	Lenovo	89741
1003	Acer	65012
1004	Lenovo	88056

1005	Apple	95014
1006	Sony	60601

…..

Postal Code	Customer City
30303	Denver
89741	Seattle
65012	Austin
88056	Miami
95014	Cupertino
60601	Chicago

…..

Customer ID	Employee ID
1001	003
1002	003
1003	004
1004	004
1005	004
1006	005

…..

Employee ID	Sales Person	Sales Office
003	Homes	Atlanta
004	Chin	Miami

005	Doyle	Boston

.....

Database Problem Areas

I personally did not run into a lot of problems with database design. I worked with two DBA's who were quite excellent.

Larger departments will tend to have at least one database administrator (DBA). This person works with the databases nearly every day and is normally very well trained in making them efficient. (DBA's work in an application for databases that allows them to adjust the database so it works as fast and efficiently as possible.) As such, problems with database normalization tend not to occur frequently unless it becomes clear in the first few days of that person's employment that "normalization" is not in their vocabulary. When this happened to us that person was gone quickly.

I am going to note here that database design is not trivial. When the bases get big, it is quite an art to get the base fully normalized. (The design document listing all the tables and the variables in them was over 100 pages long for one of the databases I used.)

Database Problems Access

By now you have probably figured out, however, that there occasionally are problems with database access. SQL is the main data access language.

> Fair warning: SQL statements are very accurate but many times they are very, very long. In such cases, with better communication, coders could find lots of help using an Access database or the SPSS application.

In two separate cases I managed to uncover two programmers working long hours to use SQL. In one of the cases I was called in to help one of the programmers. He was running about 1–2 SQL statements/database pulls per day. I went through about 30 in one day using the SPSS statistical system to produce SQL statements and do the pulls. In another case, the programmer was aghast when he found out we were also running around 30 pulls a day using the Access database system.

Alternative Solutions

The easiest solution to the access problem is simply better communication.

Note that these cases were people sitting about 50 feet away from one another. But because our training is so poor, they didn't even know there was a better way. It is no wonder that too many business managers say that IT never gets anything done.

Let us talk for a moment about the boys' club. Because formal training is not always there, many programmers end up teaching each other. Little pieces of information like "use Access to help you along with SQL" get passed along privately. That frequently leaves big holes in knowledge — often ones that go all the way up to the managers in IT departments.

Database Problems Multiple Pulls

Now one last word about accessing data from a database. There was the day that I was just asking one of the programmers how he was coping with the fact that the code called for multiple calls to the database and a large number of those were for the exact same data. He answered, "No problem." The database is very fast. I just go back to the database and pull the numbers every time I need the data, even if I pull the same data several times.

> **Note: Even though today's databases are very fast, there is nothing that can slow down a database retrieval quicker than multiple database calls for the same information if there are many users of the base at the same time.**

Say, for example, that the coding in a section calls for pulling the same data three times in about 50 lines of code. Say also that each call takes 0.1 sec. Pulling the data three times will only increase the database time to 0.3 sec.

However, if 1000 users are on the system at the exact same time (something that can be common in large companies, particularly in situations involving ATM's). Now the retrieval time is 300 seconds, or 5 minutes. Often, when a coder is writing he or she fails to think that there will be many users when the program goes live.

Solution Areas

Nicely, Java does provide ways for "caching"/preserving data so it is there each time it is needed and multiple calls are not needed.

Chapter 12: Web Sites

Although web sites have not been mentioned much until now, it is one of the places where too many software mistakes occur. It is all too often that the web sites for our local businesses are out–of–date or, better yet, simply do not go where they say they are going. Often it can end up being a surprise when you open a local restaurant web site to find the latest menu — or the latest special event (think Thanksgiving Brunch) — or directions — or times for dinner.

Problem Area: Expensive to Keep Up–To–Date

One reason local owners do not keep their sites up–to–date is Facebook. Truth be known, Facebook really is a form of "web site" **which is easy for the owner to change on their own, and does not always cost when one does it.** And that brings up the "real" problem with regular web sites and that is the price. Many small business owners simply cannot pay a couple of hundred dollars a month to a web developer to keep their sites up to date. And when you know you can change things yourself on Facebook, maybe you do not need an all–correct web site.

Alternative Solution

I do have a suggestion. A lot of people still visit web sites and they still appreciate a good web site. A good web site can position a business in a very positive way.

A friend of mine had a real estate business and needed frequent changes to the web site. (Think of pictures of the current houses for sale.) Their programmer set up the site so that changes could easily be made by swapping in and out of the site a PDF file, where the PDF file with the old set of house pictures had been updated with the new set of houses. The rest of the site remained unchanged.

What we really need — what somebody needs to write — is an **easy to change** web site. It may be done with PDF files, or it may be done in another way, but what it needs is the ability to make changes without having to pay the coder again and again. Hint: it is also the case that many small business owners do not have the money to buy into a contract which allows changes for a price.

> **What many business owners need is a way to make web site changes "For Free!" Consider the following as one idea: a package that charges to mount and maintain the site while making frequent changes easy and free or low cost.**

Problem Area: Fancy Sites

Perhaps the second biggest problem with local web sites is the "fancy" entrance to the site. I have seen some really beautiful beginnings that I have also waited a very, very long time to see.

It does make a certain amount of sense that when someone pays a lot to a developer that they be given a couple of "special" views and a "wow" beginning. Unfortunately, these local web sites take a long time to open. They also tend to frequently be called up just as one is going out the front door and the question of interest is when dinner is served and how to get to the restaurant. Waiting until breakfast for the site to open is generally not a good solution.

Alternative Solution

When I was working at the advertising agencies, it was frequently necessary to remind the creative staff that the purpose of the ad was to sell the "product", not the ad agency. Those sites which will sell the best are those which will provide the best and most information about the product in the easiest manner for the viewer.

For a restaurant, a fantastic food shot will do more instantly to sell a restaurant than the most innovative opening sequence one can develop. For other sites, consider photography which is on strategy. For example, outside gorgeous winter shots are very much in keeping with the strategy for Coors beer as cold and refreshing because it is made with Rocky Mountain spring water.

121

Problem: Leaving the Site and Going Nowhere

When one is going through the web to prepare a class paper, there is nothing more exasperating than clicking on a button which takes you to another site for additional information, only to find out that there is no way back. Now you have to recall how you got to the first site in the first place and most of the time I cannot.

It is important that I tell you that the above is a mistake I seem to regularly make when developing a new web site. It is just too easy to forget that the new page came from another page to which one frequently needs to return.

Problem: Clicking on a Button and Staying Exactly Where You Started.

Just yesterday I was in a restaurant site again and saw a list of menus I could click on. I clicked on the menu item "Dinner" and politely sat there staring at the list of menu types with which I had started.

The person standing behind me said, "What's your problem?" and scrolled down the page where we all got to see the Dinner Menu. The problem was that I could have been there a very long time before I decided to scroll down. There was no indication or arrow indicating that there was anything below the page I was on and since there are a lot of sites which have nothing below the page — you usually click somewhere to get to the next page of the site — I had no reason to scroll.

Problem: "Click on the Button", Only There's no button.

For reasons that are beyond me, this situation frequently happens with sites where it is impossible to contact a real person to get one out of this problem.

> **Missing buttons or buttons on web sites that lead nowhere (and definitely not to where they started) are extremely bothersome to most users. Most can be solved simply by having an uninterested party try out the site and have the site owner check out the site on a regular basis.**

Alternative Solutions

Fortunately, the three problems above are very easy to solve. All one needs to do is get an uninterested party to "use" the site and tell you how things are going. Even easier is using it yourself if you are the site owner. I become more and more convinced each day that all too many owners just don't go check their sites on any kind of a regular basis.

Yesterday, we hit a site that just plain didn't work at all. Oh yes, we were there because we had received the flyer in the mail announcing their Annual Fall Sale. By the way, it is also an excellent idea to check out the sites of the competition while you are doing this. And owners should be checking their own sites frequently – if only to remind them that it is Christmas time and the Spring Sale List is what is on the site.

Advertising Experimentation Days

The internet is just learning how to use advertising for the best results and the most profit. A couple of years ago, the most complicated "ad" was a 2–inch box with a simple message like "Buy XX Soda." At first the agencies found it difficult for visitors to their sites to put up with advertising similar to what is on TV. But the agencies have gotten much more experience now and they are better at being non-intrusive.

We now have "video" ads, which apparently are a full page "print" ad with no sound. Unfortunately, the visitor has to get rid of the video ad to get to the site requested, but it is not that difficult.

It is really as recently as this summer that I have begun to see some really fine advertising on web sites. I strongly suggest we give the ad guys a little bit of leeway to perfect web site advertising. It might really be worth it.

Chapter 13: Women in Computing

There is one very large pink elephant in the room. That elephant is women and why it is that we don't seem to attract very many of them to computer science. In fact, computer science almost lost me. Below will tell you a bit about my undergraduate intro to engineering.

Now, this book is supposed to be about finding where we are making mistakes in our software and how we can improve that output. The mere fact that we are not including in our software efforts approximately half of our national intelligence says more than anything about why our efforts to improve software performance may not be totally successful. Enough said.

Getting Me Educated: The Questionable Days
Would She Make It to an IT career?

I would like to start by giving you a very quick background to my early life. It should help you understand how I actually got to IT. It was definitely not a straightforward path.

I grew up in Cheyenne, Wyoming — the really big city — in Wyoming that is. And yes, I sat on a horse once. Mom was a school teacher who had moved up to elementary coordinator. My grandmother (aka Gammy) had also been a school teacher. In her days it was really unique to both have a degree and to teach. (Also from early pictures, Gammy was extraordinarily stylish.) My father disappeared from the scene about the time I was four. I did not see or talk to him until I was 17. From then on, I saw him five or six times. Missing a father in my everyday life did mean, however, that I was used to the idea of women in a full–time working role.

When it came time to consider colleges, I had one goal. (At that time, everyone was going on and on about the importance of advanced degrees.) I knew that we didn't have all the money in the world, so I decided (in my 18–year old extremely sophisticated manner) that I needed to major in something that would give me a career with *only* a bachelor's degree and no advanced training. You know, that really isn't all that easy. You quickly cut out things like history, English, chemistry, etc. Engineering was a great answer. I selected Chemical Engineering because I had liked the high school chemistry class I had.

You probably are asking yourself why I didn't select computer science. For a minute I had to think on this one. Then I realized that, in those days, computer science was not a separate department. It was frequently part of the electrical engineering department, and I was not a whiz at electrical things. Computer science also tended to be available only at the graduate level. Enough said.

I'm going to interrupt here and explain that throughout my life, I have had a propensity toward math and I really liked math. On things like PSAT's and SAT's, I would often score in the 99th percentile on the math section. *(In those days, females and males were scored separately. Females needed fewer correct answers to score at the 99th percentile.)* On the English section, I would score above average, but not near the 99%ile. My math propensity was what gave me the advantage I had. (To today's students— do you have an area where you excel? If so, go for it.)

Oh yes, did I have any idea what Chemical Engineering was? No. I hadn't even considered that part (in my 18 year–old very sophisticated way). What I did know was that my folks had taught me that anything I could dream, I could aspire to. The world had no boundaries.

Some of you are probably deciding at this point that it may not be worth your time to continue to read about the background of someone who never even bothered to learn about their chosen field. Or you may be more like me, who really can't stand those parents who tell their non–talented kids that they are fabulous regardless of how bad they are. Actually, my parents were quite good at letting me know if my plans were not going to materialize. (I do remember Mom letting me know that the dance teacher refused to have me in her class any longer because I was one bad dancer. I was seven. Kicked out at seven. Yes, there were limits on my dreams.)

The real question is how many high school grads today are as lacking in career knowledge as I was. *I am guessing that it is more than we think.*

One of my more inventive days occurred the day the recruiter from one of the Ivy institutions came to our school.

I anxiously awaited his meeting with me and our guidance counselor. I announced at the start that I would like to get my engineering degree from that Ivy school. This very polite and knowledgeable young man answered that he thought I would really enjoy getting a degree from their sister school for women. I quickly picked up the possibilities. Oh, I said, "So I can do my engineering courses at the Ivy league school but actually get the degree from the women's college. Well, he said, "not really. But you will definitely like the women's college." You can imagine how bizarre the next few minutes were but we finally settled on the idea that I could EITHER go to the women's college and not major in engineering OR – oh, seems there was not anything after the OR. . .

Both Northwestern and Cornell offered me a place in their engineering departments. I selected Northwestern with a full tuition scholarship and so looked forward to my first day of orientation. There are two days I particularly remember as an engineering student. Those two days were critical in setting my future direction. The fact that I remember so clearly these two days that happened over 50 years ago should give you a clue to their importance in cementing my STEM career.

The first day of classes I walked into quite a large classroom for the orientation. A professor walked in and said "Welcome, tech weenies and ladies." At that point, I'm guessing about 147 male faces turned toward us — the three ladies in 1966's freshman class. From that point on, we would always be "different". Maybe the prof was trying to be nice. Maybe he wasn't. But it did not help. And while we are at it, it sure does not help to refer to any engineer as a "weenie".

Three months in – I knew that STEM wasn't for me. The second day I remember so clearly was somewhere around the start of the second quarter. It was about 10:30 at night. I had been in a third floor lab in one of the engineering buildings since around seven. I remember the incredible glare from the overhead lights when I finally looked up from my work. I glanced around squinting and realized: I had been in the same room for over three hours with about 30 young single men and I had not recognized or spoken to one of them and not one of them had recognized or spoken to me. Their eyes were still very much on their papers.

Later back in the dorm, I realized that I didn't know anybody in my classes (except maybe one of the other two women). I didn't have conversations with classmates before class. I didn't do homework with anybody. I muttered "four more years of silence" and the next day I went to the Dean and dropped out of engineering. (I told you it was not going to be a straightforward path to IT.) I selected a major in psychology – I had really liked my first psych course. I did keep my minor in math.

It is only fair that I tell you now that I also had a hard time becoming a part of the university social scene. Consider that what we are talking about is a female engineering major in an age when many did not believe that females could do "science" and "math". I came on a full scholarship from a small state unfamiliar to many of the students. I was not pledged. There was not a perfect fit, shall we say, with my classmates who were normally referred to as nouveau riche.

Back to engineering, the Dean suggested that they really didn't want me to drop the engineering major — I had the highest first quarter average of any of the new class. I screamed "people — I need people. I must have people." And in psychology I found them. By the end of the year there were about 12 of us who studied together; went to class together; and went to the Grill after class together. These were people who would become long–term friends.

One advantage psychology had was an early course in Experimental Psychology. This was a small class, taught by a senior professor, and it required us to work in teams to actually carry out a research project. You really got an idea of what the career would involve.

Almost most important: the course did allow everybody to get to know each other and become friends.

An additional happening occurred to influence my career — my course in ALGOL. ALGOL was one of the new computer languages. Our prof had just been through a class and had notes, but no one had written a book yet. (We really were in the early days of computing and we all tried to share what we were learning.) I stayed in the class for about three weeks and then I went to the prof and explained that while I was getting the assignments done by "copying", I really didn't understand what the statements meant. Again, the prof noted she didn't want me to quit, because I had the best mid–term grade in the class, but I did quit because I was not learning, I was copying. This class probably moved me a little further away from that career in IT.

Graduate School: The Good Days with Money

No sooner had I blinked than it was time to graduate. Oops, I had dropped out of the career that could get one hired with only a BA. Fortunately, in the end for all of us, about that time (October 5, 1957) the Russians placed a satellite in orbit called Sputnik. Americans responded very quickly. Following their victories in WWII, Americans who had always been first in everything and especially science, panicked. This just couldn't be happening. Sputnik dramatically underscored in America the need for improving science education and basic research. In the year before Sputnik, The National Science Foundation's appropriation was $40 million. The year after Sputnik, it more than tripled to $136 million.

https://www.nsf.gov/about/history/nsf50/nsf8816.jsp

In addition, very soon the Congress passed NDEA Title IV whose purpose was to provide more college teachers. They knew that due to the baby boom we would soon need them.

I heard there was money. Excellent! About this time, one of the psych professors happened to look down and see the schools to which I was going to apply for graduate school. He noted that I had listed two of the most competitive, cut–throat institutions. He suggested that in addition to the cut–throat schools, I should consider a couple of schools with excellent reputations but without the cut–throat atmosphere. One question you may be asking is whether expectations for me were being set just a little lower by ones who cared for me. Guess what, though. This particular prof was absolutely right. I was so much happier under less stress.

My graduate years were paid for by an NDEA Title IV Fellowship.

Title IV of the National Defense Education Act (NDEA), passed in 1958, was intended to alleviate an existing and projected shortage of qualified college teachers. This was to be accomplished by means of awarding 3–year fellowships for full–time study to doctoral candidates interested in college teaching, by institutional allowances for strengthening graduate programs, and by a wider geographical distribution of strong graduate programs.

http://eric.ed.gov/?id=ED054739)

Please note though that I had not applied for an "engineering" type graduate program. But somehow, engineering was there to tempt me again. Coming back from my application to Colorado was the announcement of a brand new program in Quantitative Psychology. The program featured training in statistics and experimental design, and most important, they featured computer training and the use of their own computer in the Quantitative Psychology department. There were four of us in this brand new program. I had a wonderful time at CU and felt very much at home. CU had and still has an excellent graduate psychology program. I am very proud of my degrees from CU.

The classes I took would end up being "right on" when it came to prepping me for the several STEM careers I would have after school.

• **The psychology section** had the usual courses at the time in learning theory, experimental design, and basics such as the psychological statistics course all psych grads took.

• **The "quantitative" section included factor analysis and multivariate statistics/analysis. In addition, quantitative students** also took the statistics course given in the engineering school which included, much to our consternation, tons of calculus. (The professor was always there to give us a break on the calculus. We would get credit for solving the stat part even if we didn't quite get the calculus part. Thank you. Thank you.)

• **The computing section** included the basic Introduction to the Computer three courses given in the engineering school. In addition, and ahead of their time, the psych department taught Fortran Programming as part of the graduate statistics course. I would end up teaching that Fortran course after taking it myself.

To give you a bit of a feel for the real inside of academics, let me tell you about the questioning some of us graduate students received during a site visit for a grant application. There seemed to be universal agreement among members of the site committee that our graduate curriculum was far too "broad" in scope to prepare future academic researchers in a specific area. *(Please note that later, that "broad" curriculum would become the lifesaver for the different STEM careers in which I ultimately engaged. On the other hand, that broad curriculum was not helpful in terms of getting me out front with several publications while still in grad school and prepping me for an academic career. You may wish to read the above sentences very carefully.)*

We were very fortunate. The program in Quantitative Psychology at the University of Colorado had its own mini–computer, the Xerox Sigma 3. Keep in mind this was 1964. This was *definitely* not common. Plus, the university had one of the largest computers of its day — the CDC 6600. *(The big computer was needed for work at the National Center for Atmospheric Research — NCAR.)*

In addition, one of the highlights of the program was the summer I spent as the lab technician for a program — CLIPR — the Computer Laboratory for Instruction in Psychological Research. Our lab had two of the newest mini–computers, an IBM 1130 and a PDP–8, plus teletypes to the IBM 7094. We were truly at the forefront of computer science.

Some days were, of course, better than others. On my list of "clumsy days" I include the day I hit something wrong and ended up having to reload memory for the IBM 1130 in hexadecimal. Even better was the day when one of the tape reels on the PDP–8 managed to escape its plastic boundaries (well, I may have had a little something to do with it). I ended up chin–high in ½ inch tape off the reels, and I mean chin–high. But other days were quite a bit better.

On a more serious side, my dissertation was a statistical model (a Markov Model of two–stage learning). I ran — common for its day — a learning experiment and gathered data on how long it took respondents to learn my task. After gathering all the data, the next step was to go back to the model and to solve for the value of the main variables in the model using the data from the experiment. I used a program called Simplex on the university mainframe, the CDC 6600.

I knew I was at the forefront when I re–ran the program a year later under double precision at NYU (numbers were stored at double the usual number of bits) on the Univac 1108 (at that point one of the largest computers in the world). The Univac was slightly larger than the CDC 6600 in single precision. I got two different answers, indicating we were running the upper limits of the two machines. Fortunately, the psychological outcome did not change, but it did make me appreciate more where I was and where I had been.

Perhaps the most important part of my graduate training was learning Fortran, the computer language used for almost all scientific programming in the 1960's and 1970's. Fortran is still used today for large scale, mainframe programming, especially parallel processing super computers. The head of the Quantitative Psych Department, Dr. Daniel E. Bailey, had just written a superb book on Fortran Programming. Later in my graduate years, I would teach the Fortran course.

Hopefully, the one thing that should have come through in my descriptions was how exciting it was to be a part of the very latest in research and development. I'm not sure it mattered what the exact topic or subject matter was. The important thing was to be at the forefront of the work.

One strange action: I was the only one in the psych doctoral programs to get a Master's degree. By the late 1960's, concern was rising in academic circles about budget cuts. My professors suggested getting an M.A. on the way to a Ph.D. as a safeguard against funding failures. Yes, they were looking out for me.

The Not So Good Days

While the NDEA fellowship had as its goal making more college teachers, by the time I got to the fourth year, the program had worked so well, along with other like programs, that we had a Ph.D. Glut in the U.S.

Thanks to my dissertation chairman, Dr. Walter Kintsch, I had two interviews for a faculty position. In both cases, I visited the campus, spent overnight there, toured the campus, and met the faculty and had dinner with them. I also gave a seminar based on my dissertation.

The big attraction of NYU was its Univac 1108. Less of an attraction was the fact that when I arrived for the job interview in late winter, the temperature inside the university buildings was roughly equal to the inside of a well–stocked meat locker. It seems the heating and energy folk for the university were on strike. It remained cold the entire time I was there. Fortunately, that was the last time while I was at NYU that that situation occurred.

I did accept a tenure–track position at the University Heights campus of NYU in the Bronx. (Think about this:

this naïve kid from Cheyenne Wyoming accepts a job at a school with freezing buildings in the middle of what folks back home thought was the "big" and "dangerous" city. Some would call that stepping outside the box.)

As I arrived, the University had just finished a review of faculty salaries and "Surprise!" the women faculty made less than the male faculty. In an attempt to make the averages closer to equal, the university decided to give a $2,000 raise to the women Assistant Professors and nothing to the men. That meant that for my second and third years, I made $13,000 while my two best faculty friends (one later to become my husband) made $11,000. May I humbly suggest that this is not the way to equalize salaries.

Things would change very quickly after that. Within a week of getting my new office, I picked up the school newspaper and read the following headline: "NYU going bankrupt. To sell the Heights campus to the City University of New York." Needless to say, the next two and a half years on the Heights campus were somewhat nervous as we went from one rumor to the next. After a couple of late paychecks, we added the worry of when we would be getting paid, period. Fortunately, this late pay problem was short lived (only a few months) with the exception of problems with a couple of grants. In the long run, those of us remaining at the Heights were transferred to NYU's Greenwich Village campus.

I can't say we received terribly warm welcomes as new faculty members on the Manhattan campus. I did get a lab for my experiments, but they forgot to put any furniture in it. About my office, on the other hand, it was explained to me that a graduate student was currently occupying the space and it would be good idea if we didn't force him to move offices before he got his degree. They would give me a temp office until then. I explained that given I had just gotten out of the hospital with a slipped disk, that my moving heavy books twice might not be a good idea. I fear I did not make a lot of friends that day. (You might be interested that a male faculty member got exactly the same "office offer" as I did.)

A form of "isolation" came up again about the middle of my first year downtown. A senior faculty member told me to come down to his office. He wanted to know how my research was coming along. It sure seemed like an interrogation, as opposed to a question of whether there was any way he could help. I fumbled along with a vague answer.

The problem that I still have not solved in my own mind is the question of how much about one's research do you share with others. If you are among a group of scientists working in the same general area, then you should probably be careful not to let loose an important finding before it is published. On the other hand, this professor was not doing research directly in my area. To this day, I would love to see some discussions about this issue. (I think the professor may possibly have been trying to be of help *in addition to* checking up on me, but maybe we could have had lunch or he could have come to my office.)

Finally, shortly after we arrived at the downtown campus and to round things out, we heard that our disappearance would be most welcome, as our presence was keeping the current faculty from hiring a group of professors selected for the Grants for Excellence program.

Things became clearer as each day passed. It would be a downright excellent idea to get out of there. But where to go? One thing was very clear. At that point we didn't know if NYU's money troubles were soon going to hit a lot of universities or whether it was unique to NYU. Very fortunately, my father set me up with a conversation with one of his friends about a career in "marketing research".

We had never heard of "marketing research" as a major industry. We very quickly found that marketing research was just about the same thing as psychological experimental research. Okay, sometimes they used different words, but the activities were the same. We had a place to go.

By September of 1974, both my future husband and I were advertising researchers at two Madison Avenue advertising firms. The two companies were among the largest advertising agencies in the world at that time. These would become some of my most treasured times in the working world.

How My Education Affected My Commitment to Computer Science

The reason I went so carefully over my past education was to see if I could identify places where my decision to continue with engineering had been helped or hurt by certain circumstances. On the positive side, I noted above how incredibly important it was that I became a part of activities at the forefront of that day's knowledge and development.

On the negative side, I found it a little surprising when I looked back at my history and saw that "isolation" was such an important variable in my decisions. Actually, what I wanted was not to stand out – just to be one of the other guys. And — more important — I wanted a group of cohorts/friends. I absolutely did not want to be isolated.

It is important that math and data analysis and computing all require a lot of time alone with one's self and the numbers. Later when I was hiring personnel, one characteristic I looked for was the person who would simply get lost in the numbers and *forget to go home*. I remember going in to the office of a recent graduate whom I had just hired. It was 7 p.m. and, apparently, he had forgotten to go home. He was just deep into the numbers. That's the kind of a person who will really be satisfied with a data analysis and computing career.

That however, is completely different from not having cohorts to work with and talk to when you aren't deep into the numbers. Actually it is really nice to have someone to go with you to the Grill after class. As I said in the main section, now that there are more women in software engineering — we're up to around 20% now — it is less likely that a new software engineering student will face the kind of isolation I faced. I hope not. But when you are considering a school, you may want first to find out how many women will be in your class. (When I was majoring in psychology, my group of friends consisted of both men and women. It is only when the number of women is extremely small that you get isolated off to the side.)

My husband likes to point out that having significant numbers of women and minorities is important for everyone since it parallels the work environment that one is likely to work in or manage later in life.

You may also want to check the class schedules to see if there are any courses in the first year that cover the various kinds of engineering to give freshmen a better idea of what each type of engineering career will involve.

Look for a smaller class with lots of professor interaction and opportunities to work with other classmates on projects. There is one other possibility which is truly remote, but I always mention it anyway. As easy as it is to produce a U–Tube, there should be a series of CD's/U–Tube's that go through the various engineering careers. Consider this an invitation for someone to produce a set of these.

It also may be useful to check with your local school district or community college to see if any pre–college courses are being offered for topics like analytical graphics.

Finally, there is the single most important way for our society to convince more students to enter engineering. In the 1950's the Russian Sputnik convinced our legislatures to make a series of scholarships and fellowships available for those interested in science and/or engineering and (the one used for the NDEA IV Fellowships) available for those interested in teaching. Money was definitely key in guiding me and most of my friends toward careers in STEM.

Today, money is not so available so it is even more important to apply to a wide variety of institutions — selective, not so selective, public, private, etc. There are still financial aid packages that will not involve putting one $30,000–$60,000 in debt before even considering graduate school, so keep your options open and go for any appropriate scholarships you can find.

It is also important to make sure that college and engineering are really what you want. There are a series of public and private non–profit institutions that offer non–B.A. programs such as data analysis or computer programming or database administration or – on the hardware side – computer network maintenance or – on the digital manufacturing side, programs involving training in the latest digital manufacturing machines. **Community colleges are key in this arena. And please do not fall for the line that everyone in the future will need a Bachelor's degree.**

Diversity Issues: The Bad Days

As I write this, diversity issues are hitting major newspapers frequently. I need to put my two–cents in, but it is important to note that these examples are not from my time in IT. They are from my time in the advertising business — which in previous chapters I have praised so deeply. What you need to know is that these happenings occurred *after* I was promoted into the upper ranks — think Senior VP.

What this tells me, however, is that the causal factor may have been my rank – not whether it was IT or advertising or whatever. Think for a moment that the majority of women you are hearing from today are those who have moved upwards on the career ladder.

What bothers me most is that I do not have a solution to this set of problems. You will understand this below, but I really do not want to stop the boys from going on their fishing trips. I also do not want to go with them. But hey, lunch is something else.

Over the years I had worked my way up the agency ladders and it is only fair that I pass on to you some of the not so favorable happenings.

At that point I had moved up in the system. However, it was the "guys" who went to lunch together every day (and, importantly, discussed work as they ate). The "guys" also went each fall on a group fishing and camping trip. I found it interesting that they did choose to tell me about the trip because they knew I would have found out anyway. Oh yes, the agency had season tickets to the baseball team, providing excellent opportunities to get to know the clients better. When they finally invited me to a game, they explained that they thought I did not like baseball. Ah, but I do!

We also had incidents with clients and outsiders. There were two major incidents. One was the client who had their really top personnel visiting from outside the United

States. The client had not been happy that I was the research person. They had asked that I be moved off the account before they had seen any work. On the day of this visit, however, we had no one else to give the research but me. The morning session lasted 3 hours. I was 2 hours of the 3–hour presentation. Lunch time came and the males went to the (male only) private club on the top floor of our building. I went to lunch at the building's cafeteria. Later this problem became less when a couple of the high level female creatives let their feelings be known when they were kept out of the private club. (While the gender exclusive clubs are no longer a problem, other visible career impediments are still present.)

The second incident occurred as part of a planning meeting for a major professional organization. The meeting was set up at a private men's club. It was explained to me that there were two doors to the club — one for men and one for women. When I arrived, the women's door was locked. I do remember striding back to the agency, straight–faced and all. I called the club when I got back to my desk. It was explained to me that it was all right for a woman to go through the men's door. I walked back and joined the meeting. The apologies were sparse. Interestingly, that also seemed to stop my upward movement within the organization. I'm not sure it was them or me.

When I told the above story to a friend and suggested that I was going to put the incident in my book, the first words out of his mouth were, "But that doesn't happen anymore does it?" The implication was that no one would want to hear the story because it was "old news".

Articles in the New York Times very recently have led me to believe that at least some similar incidents are still going on — not in private clubs — but in the day to day way in which women and minorities in tech are treated.

So where do we go from here? There is the old saying that "there is safety in numbers." If we get more women and minorities into tech and into the higher levels, it should become harder and harder to carry on the old boys' club ways.

Post Thoughts

I don't want to leave this section without a couple of words on what made the ad world so great. Incredibly important was the organizational structure of the agencies. The organization of the typical ad agency then was the pure pyramidal structure used in most corporations in the 1950's to 1980's. Two positions reported to one position above the two.

This structure led to two incredibly important advantages. First, there was a structure for promotions. You knew what you were trying to accomplish and for whom you were going to accomplish it. It gave you something to work for. Second, the culture and the knowledge held within the organization was passed on through each structure so that a boss knew what his subordinates knew and the subordinates would come to know all that a boss knew.

I distinctly remember one of the senior ad guys noting for me that if the sales data differed from the consumer research data, he would always depend on the sales data. He was absolutely right. And, that information does not appear in text books. You learn it directly from your boss — unless you really don't have a direct boss that you see.

Today in many software programming groups the bosses do not know how to program in the language being used and as such, have very little idea what their subordinates are doing. This also makes it much more difficult to know who should be promoted. In one of my IT positions, there were over 60 reports to one boss and you can probably guess that there also were no promotions in my time there.

The flat management style present today has drawbacks that may inhibit development of technical and career skills which may be a significant problem in IT.

At the ad agencies in the 1950's to 1980's, we worked together as teams involving management personnel, researchers, media experts, and creatives. Each of us had a specific expertise. And, in addition we had a culture and the advertising business had a huge basic research backlog to lead us. (Thank you David Ogilvy.) We also had management backing us. I will never forget the night before I was to give a research presentation based on results I had only received a day or two before. Next thing I knew the head of the office was down the hall helping to make my charts. I will never forget it.

What I have not mentioned is the one regular activity which I feel took us to the heights of excellence. **Before we would have a meeting as a group with one of our clients, it was standard procedure to meet to discuss what "our"**

point of view was to be in the meeting. We went over all the possible arguments for different points of view so we could verbalize why our view was best. In addition, we went over the response that we expected from the client for each point of view. Then we went over how we would respond to the client. When we got to the meeting, every one of us appeared well prepared. Any one of us could talk because we knew what we were to say.

Yes, those days were ones that helped us develop job and interpersonal skills which would pay off greatly as the years went by.

Chapter 14: Review — Why Too Much of our Software Has Glitches

Below are the problem areas referenced in each chapter. It can be used as a review of where we have been. The next chapter will pull together these problems and provide a set of conclusions for 1) overall, where our major problems come from and 2) how can we address these major areas.

CHAPTER 3

Problem: Basically we have too many complicated languages. We waste too much time correcting punctuation, which in many cases is the only difference between some statements in different languages. We end up focusing on the grammar rather than the function of the code.

CHAPTER 3

Problem, Extended: To repeat, we have too many languages. The vast number alone makes it difficult for computer science departments to control what languages are actually being used.

CHAPTER 3

The too many languages problem gets even worse when programs need to be updated and no one still working in the department knows that an additional language is hiding in the code.

CHAPTER 4

Problem: The hard part these days is to find a way to get our kids exposed to good programming courses. The best estimate is that 90% of our high schools don't teach computer programming.

CHAPTER 4

Problem: The major language developers — Microsoft and Sun Java —— have not in general been at the forefront in providing courses for students to learn these languages. It is very difficult in the U.S. to find individual courses in the major computer languages.

CHAPTER 5

Problem: When more than a few contract company recruiters lack skills in computer science and programming and they are the ones selecting prospects for open positions, it becomes just that much more difficult for a prospect trained in an American college or vocational institution to get an IT job and that much more difficult for the employer to hire the best prospect.

CHAPTER 5

Problem: Because many companies tend to resist hiring directly unless the prospect has just completed a bachelor's degree or above from a research university, a prospect without that degree will likely have a very small chance of being hired directly by that company.

CHAPTER 5

Problem: All along, one of the biggest problems in getting hired for an IT job has been a hesitance on the part of contract company recruiters to recommend anyone for a position the prospect has not previously held. This can be a particularly serious problem for those going after their first job.

CHAPER 5

Problem: Often one corporation may give one job contract to as many as ten or more contracting firms. If too many recruiting firms/ contracting firms are carrying the same job, it is easy to get misled into thinking the market is hotter than it is. This practice in recruiting may also have caused and may still be causing overestimates in the number of IT positions listed by groups like the Labor Department.

CHAPTER 5

Problem: If you are asked to interview with the "programming team", be aware that your chances of being hired might be very, very small unless you are demographically similar to "the team". In my experience, that most frequently translates to a 20–29 year–old male.

CHAPTER 5

Problem: In my experience, due to Department of Labor recommendations and lawsuit outcomes, most companies would allow contract workers to only work for a firm for two years.

CHAPTER 5

Problem: Almost by definition, and due in part to lawsuit outcomes and federal directives on contract workers, contract workers in the past tended to be employed for two years and then were unemployed for the next six months while they looked for the next contract position.

CHAPTER 5

Problem: There's one other exasperating problem for a person getting an IT job. That problem is the large number of H–1B's standing in line in front of them (i.e., foreign workers hired when US. workers are supposedly not available).

CHAPTER 5

U.S. companies who work with H–1B's frequently have contracts with programming and recruiting firms that specialize in providing H–1B labor. These programming/recruiting firms push for additional slots for their foreign personnel.

CHAPTER 6

Problem: With months between original planning for use cases, etc., and the actual code generation, the Waterfall Method may end up adding coding time simply for refreshing memories of the original planning.

CHAPTER 6

With the Waterfall Method, stakeholders do not see any code until the whole program is finished. Since this period can be months long, one possible outcome is that the situation has changed for the stakeholders and there is now little interest in this particular program or in the way the program is handled.

CHAPTER 7

Problem: Actually, looking at the number of companies for whom I worked and the number of different projects on which I worked, it is surprising that I never saw an organized list of Classes for one of these programs. I also never saw a Class reused. I never saw a Class diagram. My husband reports having had the same experiences.

CHAPTER 7

Problem: When coders make little if any use of code reuse, the more difficult it is to find code to make upgrades when they are necessary. Sloppy code organization with little code reuse is at least part of the reason for too many glitches and so many updates.

CHAPTER 7

Problem: Many courses in Object Oriented Languages do not teach you how to find or how to use a class.

CHAPTER 7

Problem: One of the biggest problems may be that we don't have enough teachers well trained in how to teach the object–oriented languages and we do not have enough who understand the implications of OOP and design in a large scale production environment.

CHAPTER 7

Problem: Some popular IDE's (Integrated Development Environments) are Eclipse, Microsoft Visual Studio, WebSphere, and Rational XDE. These IDE's will take you step by step through setting up an entire outline for a Class. My coders were way along in the coding before they ever used these outlines. And their Classes were designed in a very much linear fashion – every time they needed a particular function, they just defined another Class (i.e. selected a new outline) and used the new outline.

CHAPTER 8

Problem: Too few IT employers regularly send their personnel out for advanced training. Because languages and applications change so frequently in IT, this situation can easily lead to "holes" in training, for example, the person understands the newer security features but not database features.

CHAPTER 8

Problem: Because managers of IT areas do not always possess IT skills, programmers can code in languages not expected or in open source/free languages and the managers are not always aware this is going on. Languages can be added even in IT departments with code knowledgeable bosses simply because often the only persons to examine the code are the coding team.

CHAPTER 8

Problem: Software tends to become unmanageable when coders are using open source software (free to everyone) from the outside and not all are aware of and/or competent in the materials being used.

CHAPTER 8

Problem: Productivity may suffer due to employee surroundings at some organizations. Perhaps a little less emphasis on quarter to quarter profits and more emphasis on employee surroundings might provide positive incentives.

CHAPTER 8

Problem: Due to Department of Labor recommendations and lawsuit outcomes, many companies allowed contract workers to only work for a firm for two years without making them employees. This directive represented a good opportunity for firms to lose expertise.

CHAPTER 9

Problem: At the beginning, code that is outsourced may need to be re–written simply to conform to Java coding standards.

CHAPTER 9

Problem: Outsourced coding may need to be substantially re–written beyond just for coding standards. This will affect final costs and budgeting.

CHAPTER 9

Problem: On too many occasions, stakeholders for larger projects may feel that their input is less than optimal.

CHAPTER 9

Problem: While using IDE's (Integrated Developmental Environments) will ease the coding, many are quite sophisticated applications. There may be a need to make sure team members are skilled in the best use of the IDE. Extra training may be needed. These applications are not always easy to use to their fullest.

CHAPTER 9

Change orders may be a cause of slowdown in many projects. Some firms make it very difficult to get a change order. On the other hand, some very good firms make sure that when change is needed, it goes through easily. Change orders require balance.

CHAPTER 9

Problem: It is critical to check unit testing to make sure that it is testing whether the correct answer has been delivered. Checking to see that the code "runs" is not sufficient. New applications must get correct answers.

CHAPTER 9

Problem: What I want to emphasize is the idea that for the first round, some of these problems might not seem so serious. However, when one is on the fifteenth update, the sloppier the organization of the code, the more inefficient the design, and the weaker the documentation of the code, the more difficult it is going to be to accurately make changes.

CHAPTER 10

One present weakness of Agile Development is that it tends to provide documentation that might be described as the "bare minimum". It may be filled out further later on, if desired.

CHAPTER 10

By melding parts of the Waterfall design with parts of Agile, it may be possible for Agile to produce quite fine results, even with very large, Enterprise–wide projects.

CHAPTER 11

Fair warning: SQL statements are very accurate but many times they are very, very long. In such cases, with better communication, coders could find lots of help using an Access database or the SPSS application.

CHAPTER 11

Note: Even though today's databases are very fast, there is nothing that can slow down a database retrieval quicker than multiple database calls for the same information if there are many users of the base at the same time.

CHAPTER 12

What many business owners need is a way to make web site changes "For Free!" Consider the following as one idea: a package that charges to mount and maintain the site while making frequent changes easy and free or low cost.

CHAPTER 12

Missing buttons or buttons on web sites that lead nowhere (and definitely not to where they started) are extremely bothersome to most users. Most can be solved simply by having an uninterested party try out the site and have the site owner check out the site on a regular basis.

Chapter 15: Summary and Conclusions

This chapter is an attempt to bring together major problem areas uncovered by the step–by–step procedure and to address how we might approach those problem areas.

All the way through our tour of computer science, one major idea kept surfacing:

It is very difficult in the U.S. to find good sources for learning computer programming and other aspects of computer science. This is true both for adults and also for late children and teens.

• The best estimate is that 90% of our high schools do not teach computer programming.

• A local community college or university may offer courses in one or two languages — Java (or its variants J2EE and Java SE 6), C (or its variants C++ or C#), or VB (VB. NET or VB 6) — but many will offer this only for full–time students. Recently, some are offering a course or two in newer open source/free to everyone languages such as PHP or Python, but again these are mostly for full–time students. *(Of importance, a student who has only the open source languages under their belt may not have as strong job opportunities as one skilled in the standard older languages, such as Java — which itself is open source — or C or VB.)*

• In some cities, specialized firms who offer training for personnel in larger firms may be available. However, these courses tend to be on the expensive side and not all will offer training on an individual basis.

• For the object–oriented languages, not all teachers are prepared to teach how to define and use classes, and many will resort to a linear approach to code design with little code re–use.

Future estimates foresee broad expansion in the number of ways computer coding will be applied. The expansion will be in part due to a greater emphasis on cloud computing, the collection and storage of big data, more everyday items becoming connected to the Internet in what is commonly referred to as the "Internet of things," and the continued demand for mobile computing.

Problem Area: Difficulty in Getting Training

The major question is how this lack of training is related to greater numbers of "glitches" in our programming. One noticeable way is that too much programming these days may be self–taught, meaning that standards for writing and presenting code (e.g., Java code standard) and means of testing software may not be emphasized for the self–learner as much as they are in a formal setting.

Even more important, with a shortage in well–trained and skilled coders, there are also not enough well–trained teachers. At least some of those now teaching may well have been exposed to less than optimal training themselves, especially in object–oriented design and the definition and use of classes. One fear is that those with weaker training in object–oriented design will tend to over–emphasize linear programming in their own teaching.

Finally, languages are getting more and more complex, as are the frameworks and IDE's (Integrated Development Environments) where much coding is done these days. To my knowledge, I'm not sure there are any formal training methods for these frameworks and IDE's and perhaps there should be.

Problem Solutions: Training Sources

There are two areas where pressure may be brought to improve the current training. First, at the local level, parents and teachers need to continue to emphasize to schools and the legislatures how important it is to them that good computer training be available for their children. High schools need to know that other countries are teaching programming and if we are to succeed with the next generation of workers we need to teach programming here. **And very important, we need to make much greater use of vocational training institutions/community colleges for training computer science.**

Second, we need **to improve the training itself.** This is an area where the Silicon Valley firms can provide much needed expertise. The latest research being conducted in the computer science field may not always be at the universities. Instead, much of the really new innovation in the computer field is probably occurring in the heart of Silicon Valley in private start–ups. This is where new languages are developed — especially for the mobile field. This is where new applications galore are developed. This is where lots of hardware is developed. This is where many application frameworks are developed.

We could use some help from Silicon Valley in improving teaching training and in updating curricula in computer science. Programs can be implemented to persuade these high tech firms to provide expertise in the area of improving teacher training and curricula in the U.S.

Problem Area: Computing's Cardinal Rule

Over and over again, we found examples of coders repeating code as well as data retrieval rather than sticking to the cardinal rule that code appears once and data appears once.

> • There appears to be little code re–use when programming in the object–oriented languages. Too many times we do not see definitions of classes, class diagrams., etc. What we do see is the linear programming version where coders simply define a new class each time a function is needed (even if it is the same function used many times before).

> • We have also seen retrieving the same data from the very large databases each time the data is needed, even if it is the same data pulled many

times before in that coding segment. While the excuse is that the databases are fast enough to handle such an approach, this is not necessarily true when the number of users per time period gets high. This is frequently true for large consumer applications such as an ATM machine which can get thousands of users a minute. In this circumstance, multiple pulls from a database for the same data will really slow even the best of databases.

Problem Area: Code Reviewing

Like the first problem area above, much of the difficulty here is the result of less than optimal training.

However, it is even more important to recognize that, in all these cases, the real problems appear when changes or updates are made to the code. If one is trying to correct an error — for example, Joe's birthdate in a database is listed as 1981 instead of 1982 — the task is fairly easy if the data appears in only one place. If, on the other hand, that data appears in several identical functions, the coder must find all instances and must correct them all in an identical manner. (Think what happens when an error is made in *one correction* but not in all the rest.) When this happens, update #1 turns into update #2.

The problem is a little more elusive but a lot more harmful when working with data pulled from a database. One first needs to understand that data is often being updated within these very large databases. If the data changes, then something as simple as Total Deposits can change halfway through one person's ATM session.

One way of addressing this as a potential problem is to take the data down once and use that same data for the entire "session". Fortunately, Java for example has methods of persisting the data throughout a session.

Problem Solution: Too little Code Reuse

This problem can be at least partially solved with more emphasis on the cardinal rule of programming. One way of making the emphasis stronger is by hiring a Code Reviewer. This is a position in which the person who is *not* a member of the coding team (i.e., is not an interested party) reviews the coding from all the coding groups. The Reviewer is looking for realistic code reuse and strong organization of the code. For work with databases, the Reviewer will be looking for the number of times the same data is retrieved.

Too Many Languages

One aspect of computer science that many people may not know is the number of different languages in use today. With the growth of mobile programming, the number of languages has exploded in this area. One source notes there are now over 30 different mobile languages.

Even if we go to programming languages used for computers (pc's and also the very large mainframes), these languages, while they may not have exploded as fast in numbers, have simply become more and more complicated.

- We pointed out early that a lot of the languages had definite similarities for some of their instructions. We pointed out that some differed only in punctuation. This becomes a problem when one tries to switch from, say C to Java. One can waste a lot of time looking for that missing or out–of–place semi–colon that worked in the first language but not the second.

• Note: As we get more and more languages and applications, many are set up to make certain tasks easier to carry out. We used the Access and SPSS data windows to make it a lot easier to write SQL. This particular example tends not to cause a lot of problems because the only carryover to the existing code is the SQL.

Problem Area: Too Many Languages

On the other hand, today's internet has made finding code to carry out a lot of different tasks quite easy. Some may be in a different language. It is not difficult to copy the new code in a different language into the existing code. (It is also not that difficult to download the new language onto one's machine in order to use the new code.)

Where this becomes difficult is when updates are being made and no one knows the new language is there. Whole changes can be missed and, as a result update #2 becomes update #3.

Problem Solutions: Code Reviewer/Language Review Groups

This problem can be addressed by using a Code Reviewer, just like problem #2. The Reviewer will be looking explicitly for language changes in the midst of standard code.

The important issue here is that this problem is going to become more and more prevalent as more and more open source languages become available (that's free to everyone and may be re–distributed and modified).

This suggestion may seem a bit unexpected, but I talked earlier about the World Wide Web Consortium W3C group who oversees HTML coding for the internet. This is a voluntary group which sees to it that the language remains clear and simple and usable. Many of you may feel that it is too late to start looking at improving programming now for pc's and for mobile, but having a group to oversee the field may produce some very interesting improvements.

More Problem Areas:

Above are three major areas where making a few changes might reduce the number of "glitches". There are a lot of others that could have been mentioned such as looking to improve the hiring procedures for computer science and working to meld the positive aspects of the Waterfall and Agile design methods together. But there are probably enough suggestions above to start.

Summary

I would like to make a couple of comments in closing. One is that we — every one of us — needs to be far more aware of the incredible amount of extremely high quality, no–glitch programming that we do use every day. We need to be so much more aware of the fine work that is being done behind our backs that we never even think about or acknowledge.

If we can make things a little better, it should be all to the good. I truly hope that some of the small suggestions made here will provide the impetus for a few out there to make some small changes themselves.

I, along with others with whom I've consulted want you to know:

• We don't need or want to throw out those new languages being added to our projects. All we want is for all of us to know they are there and know how to use them.

• We don't want to make it harder to find a way to learn more languages and more application frameworks. We want to make it easier and cheaper and available to all interested.

• We don't want to force everyone to put classes in every project. We want to see classes when classes make sense.

• We don't want to force yet another overseer of our coding. We do want better communication of ways to do things.

• And finally and most important: we don't want to force anybody into software development. We do want to engage the interest of those who are curious.

Postscript for Students 1: H–1B Facts

There are a couple of remaining pink elephants in the room and this one is "one really big pink elephant." That is the question of H–1B visas. The real question is whether to recommend that students follow a computer science career path when the Bureau of Labor notes that future projections of programming jobs will be that jobs will be down 8%. This occurs because, as much as programming is going to be needed, many of the jobs will either go to H–1B's or they will go directly overseas.

In June of 2016, the New York Times ran an editorial stating that:

There is no doubt that H–1B visas — temporary work permits for especially talented foreign professionals — are instead being used by American employers to replace American workers with cheaper foreign labor. Abbott Laboratories, the health care conglomerate based in Illinois, recently became the latest large American company to use the visas in this way, following the lead of other employers, including Southern California Edison, Northeast Utilities (now Eversource Energy), Disney, Toys "R" Us and New York Life.

The visas are supposed to be used only to hire college–educated foreigners in "specialty occupations" requiring "highly specialized knowledge," and only when such hiring will not depress prevailing wages. But in many cases, laid–off American workers have been required to train their lower–paid replacements.

http://www.nytimes.com/2016/06/16/opinion/visa-abuses-harm-american-workers.html?_r=0

What makes the problem even more difficult is the fact that there really is a need for software developers with well–developed sets of skills. I like to think of programmers as similar to persons with specialized skill sets, for example, kitchen design or landscape design. In contrast, I like to think of software developers as architects who work on whole building architectural designs. While there is disagreement on whether we have a shortage of programmers, there seems to be agreement that we do need more highly skilled software developers. And, of course, to be repeated for the nth time, the skills are quite different from those for programmers, but programmer skills tend to lead into software development skills.

I have argued that in order for us to set up substantial programs for developing software developers, we should probably start by setting up programs for developing programmers. Without the latter, it is kind of like setting up a Julia Child cooking curriculum for high schoolers' first class in home economics.

There is one strong reason behind my recommendation that we continue with strong teaching programs for computer science. The reason we want to do this is to provide our kids with the background necessary to become useful adults in the future. The whole world is going digital and as a country, we are crazy if we do not give our kids a step up to conquer that world. Many other countries already have set up high school curriculums to teach programming to their kids. And what have we done? We have imported many who have been taught abroad.

Now here's the rub. We are going to see below that the H–1B's that we import are paid less than it would cost American companies to hire local programmers.

Let us look at few of the facts we need to know. First, it is all too common for the H–1B's to be described as "highly skilled". It is true that the H–1B does require a Bachelor's degree or the equivalent. The yearly quota for the H–1B for 2017 is set at 65,000. There is an additional quota of 20,000 for those with a Master's degree or above. (And something I did not know before this started: there is a special visa for "geniuses" which has no quota because there are so few that ever actually qualify.)

The most accurate descriptions I have read in articles from people who are in the know are that the H–1B's are not geniuses — they are simply "normal coders" or "journeymen techies" or "degreed workers". That, by the way, was the experience I had. The H–1B's with whom I worked in the United States were on a par with the standard American programmers. Some were excellent. Some were more on the average side.

Second, the rules for H–1B visas state that they must be for technical positions for which there is no comparable U.S. citizen available and the position must pay the prevailing wage or higher.

Where the Secretary of Labor uses a survey to determine the prevailing wage, each wage range can be divided into four levels. The company using the visa can determine which level to use for a specific employee. It is interesting that many of the entering H–1B's enter at the bottom level. According to the Economic Policy Institute, 80% of H–1B holders are approved to be hired at wages below those paid to American born workers for comparable positions.

http://www.motherjones.com/politics/2013/02/silicon-valley-h1b-visas-hurt-tech-workers

As an example, according to the Bureau of Labor Statistics, the mean wage for a programmer in Charlotte, NC is $73,965. But the level 1 prevailing wage is $50,170. Most prevailing wage claims on H–1B applications use the level 1 wage, driving down the cost of labor in this instance by nearly a third. To continue, by offering $50,170 to a prospective programmer raises the possibility that they will not find a local prospect willing to take below $73,000, thereby meeting the H–1B requirement.

http://www.cringely.com/2012/10/23/what-americans-dont-know-about-h-1b-visas-could-hurt-us-all/

And third, we frequently hear that we need as many entrepreneurs as we can get to develop the exciting new products we need to compete in today's world. We want to encourage entrepreneurs to come to the U.S. and start their own business. Of interest, H–1B's do not have anything to do with staying in the U.S., becoming a citizen, or starting a business. First, the H–1B must have a sponsor who gives them a job. They cannot go out and start a business. Tata and Infosys together hired nearly half of the H–1B's last year, and less than 3% of them applied to become permanent residents. We surmise that most went home.

The one last thing to remember is that the best estimate I could come up with is that H–1B's comprise only 20% of the domestic IT workforce.

http://www.cringely.com/2012/10/23/what-americans-dont-know-about-h-1b-visas-could-hurt-us-all/

As such, I come out with the following advice: if you are really good at IT things, including programming, take a chance, and do your best to get a good grounding in software development. (Note that the Bureau of Labor Statistics lists only a Bachelor's degree for software developer — no need for an advanced degree – see Judy's life in Chapter 9.) If, in addition, you have acquired an additional skill set, such as data analysis, that skill set may get you a very good job.

Postscript for Students 2: Careers in Computer Science

Programmer/Analyst

This chapter is about the different types of background needed for a computer programmer and software developer. The entry level for a computer programmer is normally listed as a Bachelor's Degree.

According to the Bureau of Labor Statistics:

"Computer programmers write and test code that allows computer applications and software programs to function properly. They turn the program designs created by software developers and engineers into instructions that a computer can follow. Most programmers specialize in a few programming languages. Computer programmers write and test code that allows computer applications and software programs to function properly. They turn the program designs created by software developers and engineers into instructions that a computer can follow.

"The median 2015 salary was $79,530. Most computer programmers have a bachelor's degree; however, some employers hire workers with an associate's degree. Employment of computer programmers is projected to decline 8 percent from 2014 to 2024. Computer programming can be done from anywhere in the world, so companies sometimes hire programmers in countries where wages are lower."

"**Software developers** are the creative minds behind computer programs. Some develop the applications that allow people to do specific tasks on a computer or another device. Others develop the underlying systems that run the devices or that control networks. Many software developers work for firms that deal in computer systems design and related services or for software publishers. Software developers usually have a bachelor's degree in computer science and strong computer programming skills.

"The median annual wage for software developers was $100,690 in May 2015. Employment of software developers is projected to grow 17 percent from 2014 to 2024, much faster than the average for all occupations. The main reason for the rapid growth is a large increase in the demand for computer software."

"**Web developers** design and create websites. They are responsible for the look of the site. They are also responsible for the site's technical aspects, such as its performance and capacity, which are measures of a website's speed and how much traffic the site can handle. In addition, web developers may create content for the site. About 1 in 7 of web developers were self–employed in 2014. Non–self–employed developers work primarily in the computer systems design and related services industry. The typical education needed to become a web developer is an associate's degree in web design or related field. Web developers need knowledge of both programming and graphic design."

"The median annual wage for web developers was $64,970 in May 2015. Employment of web developers is projected to grow 27 percent from 2014 to 2024, much faster than the average for all occupations. Demand will be driven by the growing popularity of mobile devices and ecommerce."

Postscript for Students 3: Software Development

When looking at **all computer and information technology occupations**, it is important, as well as interesting, to note that none say there is "on the job training." Employment of [all] computer and information technology occupations is projected to grow 12 percent from 2014 to 2024, faster than the average for all occupations. These occupations are expected to add about 488,500 new jobs, from about 3.9 million jobs to about 4.4 million jobs from 2014 to 2024, in part due to a greater emphasis on cloud computing, the collection and storage of big data, more everyday items becoming connected to the Internet in what is commonly referred to as the "Internet of things," and the continued demand for mobile computing.

The median annual wage for computer and information technology occupations was $81,430 in May 2015, which was higher than the median annual wage for all occupations of $36,200.

If you search the internet for "Bureau of Labor Statistics/Computer and Information Technology" you can also look at descriptions for other occupations:

- Computer and information research scientists ($110,620, doctoral degree,)

• Information Security Analysts ($90,120, Bachelor's degree)

• Database administrators ($81,710, Bachelor's degree)

• Computer and support specialists ($51,470, A Bachelor's degree is required for some but an associate's degree or postsecondary classes may be enough for others.)

A Note on Terminology/Job Titles

There was a very good reason I selected to go directly to the Bureau of Labor Statistics. Unfortunately, over time the job titles have changed, here and there, as the field matured. The titles above used today, however, seem to fit pretty well the actual duties of the jobs. They did not always fit well in the past.

Originally there was a lot of confusion between the coder/programmers and the software developers. As a result, the outside world failed to see a difference between the two and — as a result — may have downgraded the entire field.

Yes, there is a really big difference between the two. Programmers write code, and they normally have a standard code that they must follow (including such things as capitalization, punctuation, indentation, etc.). But before they can write that code, they need a lot of input from the software developers. This includes a list of classes/functions and for each class, such details as the package name, whether the class is public, whether a main method is needed, whether class features are public or private, etc.

Below are additional items the software developers need to give the coders when you are using a popular program Rational UML (Unified Modeling Language) with which I worked.

• **Vision Statement**. The team normally starts with a "vision statement", which basically details what the programming needs to accomplish. It states the problem, identifies users/stakeholders, and spells out features of the system. It should be easy for anybody to understand.

• **List of Classes**. The next two steps can go in either order. One, you can start with the vision statement and identify nouns which can become the classes. The adjectives for a noun will become the class features and the verbs for each chosen noun will become the class functions. (For this option, see Chapter 3.)

• **Use Cases**. Alternatively, you can start with the vision statement and identify verbs, each of which — each function — can become a use case.

For each function/method defined above, designers will then write a "use case". Use cases lay out every detail that could occur and how to deal with it when you are carrying out that function/method. For example, with getFoodBuy, the use case details what should happen if a customer decides not to purchase a food item that they have already picked up, or if they try to return an item. This is all written in English but serves for the programmers as directions for coding.

A use case should provide the flow of events. There will usually be one basic flow — customer buys item — and one or more alternative flows — buyer returns the item. The case should include preconditions, things which must be true before the case begins. The case will also include post conditions, things which must be true when the case ends.

And to repeat, once the use cases are completed, nouns in the use case can become the classes, the verbs become the functions, and the adjectives become the class features.

• **Activity Diagrams**. The last two development items look at the flow of events. An activity diagram can be developed for every basic flow from a use case and also for important alternate flows. Rational provides a program which uses specific symbols to lay out the flow. For those of you who came into programming early, the activity diagrams look suspiciously like what we used to call flow charts. They are critical to the success of most really good coders.

• **Sequence Diagrams**. The same is almost true of "sequence diagrams" which lay out (here you need to look to Rational) the sequence of each event in the basic flow (and important alternate flows).

Now you see why a Bachelor's Degree is needed for software development. It does require a specialized skill set, but it is a challenging career that is also most lucrative.

We've pointed out that computer programmer is an excellent starting point for a career in computer science. With more education, the next step is to become a software developer. As the programs become bigger and more complicated, these become quite challenging careers, plus a lot of fun. The question, the one we started this postscript with, is whether to recommend such a career when the starting point is predicted to lose jobs over the next decade.

The one reason why the jobs are sent overseas or given to H–1B's is to lower costs for the hiring firms. However, there is a natural stopping point to such an approach. Many of the H–1B's I worked with also sent home money to their parents. They also found that living in the U.S. was a lot more expensive than it appeared at first. I remember the day that one of the guys found out that, in addition to his auto insurance and health insurance, he was also going to have to get apartment insurance. He was not going to need such a package at home in India. Yes, theoretically there should be an end point for reducing wages in the U.S. for H–1B's.

My guess is that the salaries for the H–1B's here now have about reached as low as they can get and still provide an incentive for taking on an H–1B job. (Yes, coders can still be hired for even less if they stay in a country other than the U.S. But there will still be a need in the U.S. for the more skilled programmers.)

In summary, so long as you do not enter the field with the assumption that you can get one of those outrageously high salaries that tend to appear in the news, you should be fine. There are still very good compensation packages in the field. All in all, if this is an area in which you do well, I'd say:

Go for it!

About the Author

Judy grew up in Cheyenne, WY. She was introduced to computer science and engineering during her undergraduate work at Northwestern University in Evanston, IL. In 1966, she received her B.A., although she had made an early switch to a major in psychology (looking for more social interaction) while retaining a minor in mathematics. Her advanced degrees, however, directed her back toward computer science. She received an M.A. in 1969 and a Ph.D. in 1971 from the University of Colorado at Boulder, majoring in Quantitative Psychology (1/3 computer science, 1/3 experimental psychology and 1/3 statistics).

Judy started her working career as a Tenure Track Assistant Professor at New York University where she met her future husband, Frank Schapiro, who had received his doctorate from Cornell in Human Factors engineering. Due to financial difficulties at NYU, however, a career change was in the offing for both of them. Mid–career saw both Judy and Frank enjoying positions in advertising and marketing research at leading U.S. advertising agencies and corporations.

In 1985, Frank started Demand Factors, Inc., an independent marketing research and planning firm with an emphasis in multivariate statistics and big data analysis. Judy joined him in the business shortly thereafter. The business was heavily involved with organizations working to strengthen America's manufacturing arm and helping to keep jobs in America.

Her last positions took full advantage of her high–tech background. Following advanced training in multiple computer areas (websites, databases, programming) she was a contract worker holding the positions of senior programmer/analyst, requirements lead, and IT project manager at three larger corporations.

She and Frank are now in semi–retirement, but keep busy with two websites, http://ourchildrensladder.com/ whose purpose is to help today's kids climb higher in life and http://ludewighouse.com/index.html, the story of their restoration of a Victorian townhouse in St. Louis, Missouri. Together, in 2015, they published "The Get Real Guide to Retirement: The Balanced, Down–to—Earth Guide to a Rewarding and Happy Retirement."

www.ingramcontent.com/pod-product-compliance
Lightning Source LLC
Chambersburg PA
CBHW031957190326
41520CB00007B/277

* 9 7 8 0 9 8 6 4 2 1 2 3 5 *